"Noah St. John helped me gain the mental edge I was looking for. His methods helped me perform at my highest level without strain, and I saw better results immediately using his system."

—Andre Branch, NFL Football Player

"Before being coached by Noah, I was holding myself back out of fear. Since working with Noah, I've built a multi-million dollar company in less than two years. I highly recommend coaching with Noah, because I guarantee it will change your life, like it changed mine!"

—Tim Taylor, Real Estate Professional

"Noah St. John has been at the forefront of the business coaching industry for more than two decades now. He's the best in the business when it comes to helping entrepreneurs skyrocket their results in record time. If you want to take your business to a whole new level without the stress or overwhelm, hire Noah St. John TODAY. You'll be glad you did!"

—Anik Singal, Lurn.com 8-Figure CEO

T0036927

THE 7-FIGURE LIFE

HOW TO **LEVERAGE** THE
4 FOCUS FACTORS
FOR MORE WEALTH
AND HAPPINESS

DR. NOAH ST. JOHN

MEDIA

Published 2023 by Gildan Media LLC
aka G&D Media
www.GandDmedia.com

FIRST EDITION: 2023

Front cover design by Tom McKeveny

Library of Congress Cataloging-in-Publication Data is available upon request

ISBN: 978-1-7225-1074-9

10 9 8 7 6 5 4 3 2 1

This book is dedicated to #Afformers and
#AfformationWarriors around the world:
Those brave souls who ask better questions
to make this a better world
for all of God's creatures.
And to my beautiful wife, Babette,
for being the best example of a Loving Mirror
I've ever met.

Contents

Introduction

Have you ever dreamt of living The 7-Figure Life? Have you imagined what it would be like to live without constant financial stress, knowing that you can easily afford your lifestyle and contribute to the charities and causes that are important to you?

Have you imagined what it would be like to have the freedom to pursue the career or start the business that is most in line with your purpose and your values? Have you dreamed about living where you want, in the house of your dreams, all while having the time to create lasting, positive memories with those you love?

For many, such dreams are just that—fantasies that temporarily fill their minds and then quickly escape as they return to the real world of making a living. Often they are struggling to get by in a job that is unfulfilling. Some may entertain such dreams while running a business of their own that consumes every moment as they work hard to stay barely profitable. They end up sacrificing the relationships that are most important to them.

Even some who have reached the 7-figure range find themselves with a highly complex life, distant relationships, and a calendar that leaves them no time for enjoyment. They wonder, is this all there is?

EVEN HIGHLY SUCCESSFUL PEOPLE SOMETIMES WONDER, "IS THIS ALL THERE IS?"

If you see yourself in any of these situations, this is the book for you. It will introduce you to a set of powerful philosophies, strategies, and exercises for achieving The 7-Figure Life with more fulfillment and freedom than you ever thought possible. You'll learn them from the man known worldwide as the millionaire habits coach and the mental health coach to the stars—Dr. Noah St. John.

Noah has made a career working with Hollywood celebrities, CEOs of eight-figure companies, professional athletes, top executives, and entrepreneurs. He's the author of seventeen books including the best-selling *Afformations*. He's spoken at events across the globe and has impacted over 1.8 million people with his methods.

Noah is a coach and mentor, working one-on-one with the top 1 percent of achievers. By following his legendary methods, his coaching clients have added more than $2.8 billion in sales since 1997. But the thing that most excites him is coaching everyday people to make major breakthroughs in their lives in order to achieve new levels of achievement that they thought were out of reach.

Noah himself started out dirt-poor, living in fear and constant feelings of not having enough. By applying the ideas you'll learn in this course, he achieved a 7-Figure Life, and now he's ready to show you how to do the same.

For the first time, Noah will show you how The 7-Figure Life is about more than just money. Actually, an imbalanced attention on the acquisition of money will leave you with that "is this all there is?" lament. Of course, you'll learn plenty about money as well, but this is a holistic

NOAH WILL SHOW YOU WHY THE 7-FIGURE LIFE IS ABOUT MORE THAN MONEY.

program that involves your time, relationships, and energy. Noah will show you how to integrate these four factors to reshape your relationship to money and make an impact on the rest of your life.

1

The Easy Button for Success

*The Four Focus Factors:
Time, Energy, Relationships,
and Money*

I grew up poor in a rich neighborhood. I was raised in a little town called Kennebunkport, Maine, which happens to be one of the wealthiest communities in New England, but my family was dirt-poor. I mean that literally, because we lived at the bottom of a dirt road in a drafty, unfinished house that my parents ended up losing to foreclosure. From a very young age, I was painfully exposed to the chasm between the haves and the have-nots: the haves were everyone else in the community; the have-nots were my family.

Growing Up Poor In A Rich Neighborhood

I'm sure you've heard motivational speakers get onstage and say something like, "*We were poor, but we were happy; we didn't know we were poor.*" Well, in my family, we definitely knew we were poor! You see, my mother (bless her heart) reminded us every day that we were poor and miserable. So it wasn't happy, it sucked!

From a very young age, I hated that life of poverty, fear, and lack. I saw great wealth and abundance right down the street. So I asked, "How do I get from here to there?" But I didn't have anyone in my family that I could talk to, or any coaches or mentors.

I'm known as the nerdiest nerd in the personal and business growth industry. When there's a problem, I just can't stand it; I have to roll up my sleeves and get right down to the molecular level until it is fixed. I've always been this way. Even from a very young age, I did what we nerds like to do: I went to the library and started reading every book that I could on personal growth, self-help, and success—classic self-help authors like Dale Carnegie, Napoleon Hill, Stephen Covey, Wayne Dyer, and more. And I really tried to apply them. I read all these self-help books, but I couldn't get them to work for me. At the age of twenty-five, I was so depressed and frustrated that I decided to commit suicide.

At the very last moment, my life was spared. I was still here on the earth, but the problem was, I didn't know why. So I went on another long journey to find out. What is my purpose on the earth? I went back to the library, and this time I started reading spiritual books by authors like Neale Donald Walsch, Ernest Holmes, Barbara De Angelis, Louise Hay, Deepak Chopra, and others.

The Two Epiphanies That Changed My Life

In 1997, I had two epiphanies that changed my life and showed me my purpose here on the earth. That's when I discovered what was missing in traditional success literature—what all those gurus that I'd been studying had left out. That's when I started my company, SuccessClinic.com, in a 300-square-foot basement apartment with $800 to my name and a book about HTML. I didn't have any money. I didn't have any experience. I didn't know anything about marketing, sales, accounting, bookkeeping, or anything about how to run a business. There were no social media. There was no YouTube. None of that.

I didn't have anything going for me except one thing: a deep, burning desire to make a difference, to help people, to get my message out to the world, even though I had no idea how. I self-published a book, taught myself HTML, and put up the ugliest website you've ever seen. I went to a print shop and printed the book. I had no money, so I did it the cheapest and ugliest way: tape-bound, bound with a piece of tape.

Landing My First Publishing Deal

At that time, I was living in Amherst, Massachusetts, the main campus of the University of Massachusetts. Jack Canfield, coauthor of the Chicken Soup for the Soul series, was speaking there; he's an alumnus. I met him, and he loved my book, so he sent it to his publisher, saying, "You've got to publish Noah's book."

Jack's publisher gave me my first publishing deal. My first book came out in 1999; it's called *Permission to Succeed*. Then people would send me letters and emails about how it changed their lives. In many cases, it actually saved their lives: they were going to commit suicide, just as I'd been. They said, "I read your book, and I decided not to take my own life." So I knew I was on to something very powerful.

Even so, I still didn't know how to run a profitable business. As money would come in, I would just pour it right back into the business. I started hiring all these gurus, paying them lots of money until I found out that they're great at marketing, but they can't teach their way out of a paper bag.

AS MONEY CAME IN, I POURED IT RIGHT BACK INTO THE BUSINESS.

From Basement #1 to Basement #2

Ten years later, in 2007, I ended up in another basement. So I went from basement number one in 1997 to basement number two—my parents'—at the age of forty. I was $40,000 in debt because I followed what the gurus said. They took me in a totally wrong direction and gave me lots of bad advice, and I lost a ton of money.

My parents and friends were saying, "Noah, maybe you should give it up. Maybe you should try something else. Maybe you should get a job." Possibly a smarter person would have done that, but I said, "No, I'm not going to give up. I have something that I know helps people, because they've told me. I've just got to figure out how to make money doing it. "

I remembered, first of all—a blinding flash of the obvious—that if you keep doing the same thing, you get the same results. But I also remembered that everything you desire is on the other side of fear. There's always fear in the way; even though you want something, you also fear going after it.

The One Decision That Changed Everything

At that time, I made a decision that changed my whole life, which was to hire my first business coach.

He had gotten results not just for himself but, more importantly, for other people.

THIS DECISION CHANGED MY LIFE: FINALLY HIRING A REAL BUSINESS COACH.

This coach was very expensive, and I didn't have the money. (You can always find an excuse not to take action.) But I had nothing to show for ten years of hard work: basement one to basement two, only worse—$40,000 in debt. I didn't want to give up, but I had to do something different. I couldn't keep doing the same thing and expect different results.

So I faced and overcame my fear. People often say, "I want this, but I don't have the money. I can't afford it." That's almost always a lie that we tell ourselves. I hired that coach, and that's when everything changed for me; that's when I finally realized how to package my products and services and sell them online. Before that, I was just piecemealing it, and it wasn't working.

Then it started to work. I started to make enough money. I paid off my debts. I got out of my parents' basement. I moved to the Midwest and met my beautiful wife, Babette. I became a bestselling author for the first time. I went from basement to best seller to Barbados in twenty-four months using the system that I teach and live. The 7-Figure Life is not just talking about it; it's living it.

No Overnight Success

If you have a message or purpose, if you have something inside of you that needs to be shared with the world, don't give up, even if you've been beaten up by the world. This was not an overnight success; it was hard. I went through a lot of pain, a lot of sleepless nights, a lot of tears. But I've been able to break through and understand what the gurus didn't teach, and that's how I've created my niche. Unfortunately, many people have been beaten up by these guys, and I have to clean up after them. At this point, I'm like the Internet marketing cleanup crew.

Two things helped me get through that tough time. One was getting feedback from people who said, "You changed my life." I did have positive feedback from customers and clients, even though I was not doing a good job of packaging myself and selling on the Internet. This was from 1997 to 2007, when the Internet was still in its infancy. But that coach walked me through the steps for doing that, and now I'm able to walk my clients through those steps of packaging yourself.

There are three I's: you want to have greater *impact*, more *influence*, and more *income*. Impact, influence, and income. I wasn't doing a good job at any of those, because no one had taught me how. Once I discovered how to increase my impact, influence, and income, I realized that doesn't have to be as hard or complicated as the gurus make it out to be. In fact, it's crucial to keep things simple, because the old saying holds true: "Simplicity scales while complexity fails."

The second thing that motivated me was knowing that I did not want to have a job. I had worked in corporate America, and I had been suicidal. Those two things were not unrelated. When I was working at jobs, I felt as if someone's hands were around my throat all day. I was saying, "Is this it? This is the next forty years? This is what I have to look forward to? You've got to be kidding me."

Doing Whatever It Takes

I knew I couldn't go back, so it was do or die: "I will do whatever it takes to make this work, even without much success to show for it after ten long years. I know I will figure it out, because I have to."

That's what I call my *Why-To*. When you find your why, you find the way. If you don't have a Why-To, you'll quit; it's as simple as that.

My Why-To was always very strong. When I had those two epiphanies in 1997, I remember saying, "God, I don't know why you gave me these messages, but I will never quit. I will never stop till my last breath. I'm going to keep getting this message out to the best of my ability." Of course, I did not do a very good job the first ten years.

I share that story because on social media nowadays, we see a lot of so-called overnight successes: "I started my business, and three months later, I'm a millionaire." That message can work in the opposite way for a lot of people, and it can be very depressing. Some people say, "I've been at this for years, and I'm not a millionaire; I'm not successful. So I guess I'm a failure."

You're Not a Failure

No, you're not a failure. Maybe nobody has helped you yet. Maybe nobody gave you the right plan, the right tools, or the right support. When you have those three elements, you take the right actions. When you have those four things in place, transformation happens.

I had been reading those self-help books for many years, and all of them say the same thing: you've got to use affirmations. What's an affirmation? A statement of something you want to be true.

WHEN YOU HAVE THESE 4 THINGS, TRANSFORMATION HAPPENS.

When I'm speaking, I like to have everybody in the audience stand up. I say, "OK, we're going to do a traditional affirmation, just like the gurus have told us to do for decades. Everybody say, 'I am rich.'"

Everybody says, "I am rich."

You know what happens next? Everybody starts laughing. I ask, "What are you laughing at?"

"I'm not rich."

"But you just said you were."

"Yes, but I don't believe it."

Aha, see, now, that's the problem, isn't it? We say these positive statements, and we want to believe them, but nine times out of ten, we just don't. For decades, the gurus have been teaching us that if you don't believe your affirmations, just repeat them a gazillion times until you believe them someday.

That's worked fine for some people, but for most of us, it hasn't worked at all. In fact, scientific studies have shown that 75 percent of people using the old affirmations method end up more frustrated than before, because they're saying statements that they don't believe.

My Discovery of AFFORMATIONS®

For years, I was doing affirmations just like the gurus told us to do. For example, I posted notes all over my walls with positive statements like: "*I'm happy. I'm successful. I'm rich.*"

There was only one problem. The truth was that I was broke, unhappy and miserable. You can understand why I was so frustrated—my reality was very different from the statements I'd been saying for years!

One morning, in April, 1997, I was in the shower, and I was thinking about these things. "Wait a minute," I asked. "What are we talking about? We're talking about beliefs. Well, what's a belief? A belief is just a thought. What is thought?" I realized that human thought is the process of asking and searching for answers to questions.

For example, if I were to ask you this question: "*Why is the sky blue?*", your brain would immediately start to search for the answer. Even if you don't know the answer right now, your brain would automatically begin to search for the answer to the question.

So I thought, "Wait a second. If the human mind is automatically searching for answers to questions, why are we going around making statements we don't believe? Why don't we just cut out the middle man?"

If you say, "I am rich," the brain says, "Yeah, right." That's a statement. What would the question be? "Why am I so rich?" When you ask that question, your brain immediately starts to search for the answer. Psychologists have a term for this: the *embedded presupposition factor* of the brain. This is a fancy way of saying that when you ask a question, your brain searches for the answer.

So I said to myself, "Wait a minute. What are most people doing in their lives? They're asking lousy, disempowering questions like: *Why am I so stupid? Why am I so fat? Why can't I do anything right?*"

What happens when you ask lousy questions? You get lousy answers. And that creates a lousy life.

Then I thought: "What if, instead of asking lousy questions which lead to lousy answers and create a lousy life, we simply flip the whole thing on its head and start asking empowering questions, which lead to phenomenal answers and create a wonderful life?"

As I was standing there in the shower in April 1997, I said, "Holy cow! I think I just invented something." So I had to give my discovery a name, and the name I gave it was **Afformations**.

How I Invented the Word AFFORMATIONS®

How did I invent the word AFFORMATIONS? Well, one of my favorite subjects in high school was Latin because it's the source of much of our

English language today. The word *affirmation* (the old method that we've been taught for decades) comes from the Latin *firmare*, which means *to make firm*.

THIS IS HOW I INVENTED THE AFFORMATIONS® METHOD.

Now the word *Afformation* that I invented comes from the Latin *formare*, which means to *form* or *give shape to*.

Therefore, one question that I often ask audience members at my seminars is: "What if you're making something FIRM, but it's in the wrong FORM?"

When that happens, it means that you've FORMED a life that you didn't want!

For example, let's say you've been unconsciously asking disempowering questions like, "*Why am I so stupid? Why am I so fat? Why isn't my business growing?*"

What happens is that you have FORMED those questions unconsciously. The Law of Sowing and Reaping says, "As you sow, so shall you reap." However, what we're really sowing is *seeds of thought*.

When you sow lousy thought seeds, you'll end up reaping lousy results, and thereby unconsciously create a life that's not the one you really wanted.

However, using my Afformations Method, now you can start asking empowering questions, which will lead to phenomenal answers, and help you create a wonderful life!

After my discovery in The Shower That Changed Everything in April 1997, I immediately stopped using the old "affirmation" method and started to AFFORM instead. And that's when my life finally began to change for the better!

My Discovery of Success Anorexia

In October 1997, I attended a seminar on eating disorders because, as a former professional ballet dancer, I knew a lot of people who struggled with eating disorders.

As the speaker began describing people with eating disorders. I realized that I related to everything that she was saying. For example, she said that people who develop eating disorders like anorexia and bulimia are usually overachievers; they get straight A's in school; they put everyone else's needs ahead of their own, put themselves last, and have very low self-esteem.

"Oh, my gosh!" I thought. "So why didn't I develop an eating disorder?" The answer came to me immediately. I realized that women have been taught for centuries that their worth comes from their physical bodies. But men have been taught for centuries that their worth comes from their material bodies, meaning money, status, power, what they own.

Both of those beliefs are lies. It's a lie that someone's worth comes from their physical body. It's also a lie that someone's worth comes from their material body. Nevertheless, this is what both sexes have been taught for centuries. I thought, "If someone has very low self-esteem, doesn't believe in themselves, puts themselves last, and has been told that their worth comes from their physical body, doesn't it make sense they'll starve themselves of food? Hence an eating disorder.

"But what if someone has been taught for their whole lifetime that their worth comes from status, success, money, and possessions, and that person develops a negative self-image? Wouldn't it make sense that that person would starve themselves of success?"

THIS IS HOW I DISCOVERED SUCCESS ANOREXIA.

Then I realized that that was my whole life. I came up with the term *success anorexia*. I realized that this is what millions of people around the world are doing without any knowledge of it. Because no one had ever talked about it before, I decided, "This is my message." I said, "Thank you,

God; I don't know why you chose me for this message, but I'm very excited that I finally have a message."

My First Book:
Permission to Succeed ®

I went back to my 300-square-foot basement apartment and wrote my first book, *Permission to Succeed*, in just fourteen days. Because I finally realized that if we're holding ourselves back from the success we're capable of, we don't need more how-tos of success. Instead, we need to discover *how to let ourselves succeed.*

None of the self-help books that I had read had ever made that distinction. In fact, prior to my first book, every other book or seminar in personal growth was all about "how to succeed" or telling you that "you can do it."

Naturally, if you want to do something, it's good to know how to do it. For example, if you go on YouTube and type "How to make money online," you'll find a gazillion videos on that topic. If you want to know how to lose weight, you can find another gazillion videos about that, too. The same is true for thousands of other "how-to" topics you can think of.

So why isn't everyone rich, happy, and thin? Why isn't everyone a millionaire? Why isn't everyone walking around with six-pack abs? Why isn't everyone having a dream relationship? What's missing is how to *let yourself succeed*, what I call *permission to succeed*.

There are millions of us who realize, "I've been doing everything that the gurus told me; why am I still hitting this ceiling? Why am I still not able to go to that next level? Why does it always remain elusive?"

Are You Starving Yourself of Success?

Let's go back to the analogy of eating disorders. Let's say you have a person who's starving themselves of food and you want to help them. Would it actually help them if you taught them *how to eat*? "Well, first you put your fork in the food, then put the fork in your mouth, then chew and swallow your food. That's how to eat. Feel better now?"

As you can see from this ridiculous example, when someone is suffering from an eating disorder, they already know *how to eat*. So that is clearly not the problem at all.

The actual problem is that the person suffering from an eating disorder is not giving themselves *permission to eat*. People who have eating disorders are perfectly aware of how to eat. In exactly the same way, most people who have read lots of self-help books and attended lots of personal growth seminars already know *how to succeed*. Yet for millions of people, something is still missing. That's why so many people who've attended all those seminars and read all those books are still asking, "*Why do I keep hitting this plateau?*"

It's because those gurus never told you how to let yourself succeed. That's what I've been teaching for these many years. It's the main reason why my clients have added over $2.8 billion to their incomes. It's not just how to succeed; it's more about how to let yourself succeed. That is one thing that makes this incredibly powerful and life-changing. In fact, I was the first person to identify, systematize and classify *The Power Habits® System*, which is the method I use to coach individuals, groups and teams on The Power Habits® of Unconsciously Successful People.

Have you ever felt, "I've tried everything; why am I still not at the level of success I want?" Or, "Why do I keep holding myself back from the success I'm capable of?" While the gurus talk about "how to succeed," they never showed you *how to let yourself succeed*. That's one thing that makes my work different, and why my clients get such remarkable results—because even if you know "how to succeed," if you don't give yourself *Permission to Succeed®*, you'll still be holding yourself back and getting in your own way.

Indeed, one reason this system works so well is because I open the hidden "black box of success" and show you how to get out of your own way to get the results you desire. Now that's powerful!

THIS IS WHAT THE GURUS DIDN'T TELL YOU ABOUT SUCCESS.

In addition, I'm also known as the "myth buster" in the personal growth industry. To that end, let's address the myth the *comfort zone*. In fact, I've taught my clients for years that there's no such thing as a comfort zone. If that's the case, what is the truth behind the myth?

There Is No Comfort Zone

Let's say that you know you're capable of more. You know that you have a message. You know that you have a next level that you want to reach, but you're not there. Let's say that you've tried lots of different things; you've read lots of books; you've gone to every seminar. You have a lot of what I call *shelf-help*, but you're not reaching the level that you want.

Is that comfortable? No, in fact, it's decidedly uncomfortable, but it is familiar. If you look at the word *familiar*, what does it look like? The root of the word *familiar* is *family*. (In fact, one of my

first coaching clients said, "Noah, it's *family liar.*"
Isn't that interesting?) There is no such thing as
a comfort zone. What we need to look at is our
familiar zone.

The familiar zone keeps us stuck, keeps us with a
lid on our thinking. In other words, "This is who I am,
and this is what I always will be, because I don't have
any other way to get to where I want to be."

When I realized that I had discovered something
new and different in the personal growth industry,
I knew that I had to teach my methods to as many
people as possible in my lifetime. Even after more than
twenty-five years of coaching countless people around
the world, I still get excited by seeing someone's life
change, knowing that I had a part in that!

All the gurus are basically saying the same thing:
"*Work hard, hustle, grind, think positive, and believe
in yourself.*" None of what they're saying is exactly
wrong, but it doesn't quite work.

I'll give you an example. Imagine you're driving
in an unfamiliar area, and all of a sudden you realize
you're lost. For some reason, your GPS isn't working.
You're thinking, "I need to get where I'm going, but I
don't know how to get there." You see someone on the
side of the road, so you pull over and ask, "Excuse me;
can you tell me where I am?" And the person says,
"Yes, you're in a car." Now that information wasn't

wrong, but it wasn't very helpful. We see a lot of that in the self-help industry. They're telling you you're in a car when you've asked them for directions. Frankly, I started coaching out of frustration about what was missing in this industry.

The TERM Program

My 7-figure Freedom Lifestyle Formula works in four areas, what I call the *Four Focus Factors*: *time, energy, relationships,* and *money.* I love to work in acronyms, so you can just remember them as TERM. I'm going to talk about each focus factor in detail, but this is the overview: realizing that you can have more time, more energy, better relationships, and more money when you apply my formula.

Focus Factor #1: Time

The first area is *time.* Imagine having all the money in the world but no time to enjoy it. That is not what most people would call success. We help people make more in just twelve weeks than they did in the past twelve months, while gaining one to three hours per day and four to eight weeks per year.

Imagine what you did over the past twelve months. If you could accomplish that in just twelve weeks, what would that mean for you? What would that mean for your business, your life, your family, your loved ones, your legacy? It would change everything, wouldn't it? You could pay off your debts. You could perhaps buy a new house, buy a new car, and be able to spend more time with the ones you love. The value of things tends to go down over time, whereas the value of experiences tends to go up over time. To this day, my wife and I still talk about our Caribbean honeymoon; that memory grows in value over time. Whereas when you buy a thing, such as a car, its value tends to go down.

We all want nice things, but the time you spend with your loved ones is what increases in value over time. So making more in twelve weeks than you did in the past twelve months, while gaining one to three hours per day and four to eight weeks per year, is a big takeaway. That's a big promise, but we've seen it over and over again when people apply this formula. Time is the most valuable resource, because we never get any more of it. All of Bill Gates' billions can't buy one minute of yesterday.

ALL OF BILL GATES' BILLIONS CAN'T BUY ONE MINUTE OF YESTERDAY.

Focus Factor #2: Energy

The second focus factor is *energy*. Imagine if I said to you, "Okay, here's a million dollars. However, the catch is that you have to be unhappy and miserable all the time. Sound good?"

No, that doesn't sound very good at all! Because what's the point of having a lot of money if you're unhappy and miserable all the time? Therefore, the Focus Factor of Energy dictates *how* we go through our day.

When discussing energy, I'm talking about the two main types of human emotions: positive and negative. *Positive* energy means constructive emotions like happiness, joy, gratitude, love, peace of mind, and fulfillment.

On the other hand, *negative* energy means destructive emotions like jealousy, anger, hatred, envy, depression and regret. If you find that you're spending too much time in negative energy, it doesn't matter how much money you have—because you'll be living a life that doesn't make you happy.

That's why it's crucial to understand this Focus Factor, in order to ensure that you

> **IT DOESN'T MATTER HOW MUCH MONEY YOU HAVE IF YOU DON'T GET THIS RIGHT.**

create a life that gives you more positive energy than negative.

Focus Factor #3: Relationships

Now let's look at the third Focus Factor, *Relationships*. Imagine if I said to you, "Okay, here's a million dollars. However, the catch is that you have to be all alone and you get no one to share it with. Sound good?"

No, that doesn't sound very good either! Because what's the point of money if you don't have anyone to share and enjoy it with? Therefore, the Focus Factor of Relationships dictates *who* we share our lives with.

Let me give you an example. Several years ago, I took my wife on a VIP tour of the Grand Canyon. There was a private plane, a helicopter, a boat, a bus—everything. On this tour were my wife, me, and an older gentleman: just the three of us. When it was about time to get on the private plane to go back, we went to the little airport hangar at the Grand Canyon, where they have all the private planes. The older gentleman was sitting there.

I asked him, "How long have you been waiting here?"

"For about an hour."

"That's weird," I thought. "You've got the Grand Canyon here, and you're sitting in an airport hangar. Why would you do that?"

THAT'S WHEN I REALIZED THE TRUE POWER OF RELATIONSHIPS.

All of a sudden I realized why: because he had lost his wife, he had told us. I realized that what made the trip special was sharing it with my best friend, my wife. If you don't share it with somebody, it doesn't really mean anything. It doesn't have the same impact. That's when I realized the power of relationships.

Focus Factor #4: Money

Finally, there is *money*. There's a lot of what I call *head trash* about money. Just because you have more doesn't mean that someone else will have less. Another belief is that you can't be spiritual and rich at the same time or happy and rich at the same time. All of these are types of head trash that will keep you from having the money that you desire.

We must, then, consider these Four Focus Factors—time, energy, relationships, and money—in order to live what I call the *freedom lifestyle*.

Some teachers in the personal development industry insist that you need balance to feel fulfilled while being successful. Personally, I don't care about balance. All I think about is, am I happy today? Do I feel that I'm contributing today? Am I doing what I'm here on this earth to do today? Those are main questions that I ask myself each day, so I don't care about balance.

I ASK MYSELF THESE THREE QUESTIONS EVERY DAY.

However, I will say this: I learned from my father to work hard and never stop. He is the hardest-working person I've ever met. To this day, he's in his eighties; he still works and works. But my dad doesn't care about money. He is an artist, and a brilliant one. He has always been this way.

My father found his passion, and he doesn't care about money. In a way, I envy him. On the one hand, it would be nice to not care about money. On the other hand, you have to; it's something you have to focus on. Money is like a friend. If you ignore your friend, they won't be your friend for much longer. If you pay attention to your friend, they'll stay around. That's how I look at money.

Today, I turn off my computer at five or maybe six o'clock. If I'm on a podcast interview, maybe I have to go to seven or eight. In any event, I just walk away from work, because I enjoy spending time with my wife. Every night we watch TV, sit by the fireplace, relax, and talk.

This is hard for a lot of people, especially today, when more people are working from home than ever before, and it's hard to stop sometimes. But I put these boundaries in place. I don't think about balance, but I do think about boundaries.

Inner Game, Outer Game

Here is another concept that's central to my coaching and helped my clients skyrocket their success in record time. Imagine two circles; one is labeled "Inner Game," and the other is labeled "Outer Game." Where these two circles intersect is the phenomenon called "Success."

Inner Game is everything that happens between your ears. You can't see it directly, but it affects everything that you do. It includes things like your beliefs, values, desires, thoughts, priorities, and decisions. You can't see any of those things directly, but you see their effects everywhere.

Often I ask my audiences and clients, "What is one area of your life where your beliefs don't affect you?" They can't answer. Exactly: there's no place where your beliefs don't affect you. They affect your health, your wealth, your relationships, what you eat—everything.

How I Helped This CEO Quadruple His Sales

Ninety percent of the money that I've helped my clients make has come from teaching them how to master their Inner Game. I'll give you an example. I was speaking at an event in Los Angeles a few years ago, and afterward a man came up to me from the audience. He practically grabbed me by my lapel and said, "Noah, you are the coach I've been looking for. I want to hire you right now on the spot."

Now I didn't know this man from Adam (ironically, his name was Adam). I said, "What's going on?"

"Noah, I'm totally stuck. I'm only making $4 million a year."

Of course, I had to laugh. It didn't sound like much of a problem. Who wouldn't like to be stuck at $4 million a year?

He said, "Noah, I'm the CEO of a software company. And we grew to $4 million in revenues really fast, but we have been stuck at this same level for the past four years. I spent all this money on these marketing gurus, all the big names, and we're still stuck. I can't figure out why. As soon as I heard you speak about Inner Game, Outer Game, success anorexia, Afformations, and head trash, I knew that you are the coach I've been looking for."

This man hired me on the spot. I worked with him for about a year and a half. In that time, his company grew from being stuck at $4 million to over $20 million in sales in just eighteen months.

How did I help him add eight figures in less than two years? The secret is what I taught him about mastering his Inner Game. In fact, it was his Inner Game that had been holding him back.

You see, this CEO had spent hundreds of thousands of dollars on his Outer Game—marketing, sales, branding, funnels, and so on. Now there's nothing wrong with working on your Outer Game. In fact, it's essential to work on your Outer Game if you want to be successful in life and business.

However, he had plateaued precisely because no one had ever showed him how to master his Inner Game. That's what I helped him with, and that's exactly what caused his sales to skyrocket in record time.

You might say, "Well, Noah, that's fascinating, but I'm not making $4 million a year right now." The point is, I've had clients say to me, "Noah, I'm stuck. I'm only making $400,000 a year." I've had other clients say, "Noah, I'm stuck. I'm only making $40,000 a year."

You being stuck or unstuck isn't simply determined by how much money you're making right now. The fact is, you know when you're holding yourself back from the level of success you're capable of—and it doesn't feel good, does it? While Outer Game activities like marketing and sales are important, your stuckness is primarily determined by your Inner Game.

My 7-Figure Life Formula is 90 percent Inner Game. Yes, you've got to do marketing, but imagine if you are sitting there, and you have all this head trash that says, "I can't do it." You go to all these marketing gurus who are saying, "Just do it." Inside you're thinking, "I can't do it." How effective do you think that's going to be?

That's what makes my method different. In fact, this is why so many of my clients say, "Wow, I never thought of it that way before." Years ago, one of my clients said, "Noah, as we're doing this work together, it's as if you turned a light on in a room that has been dark my whole life." That's a perfect analogy.

Imagine you're in your living room when all of a sudden, someone comes in, turns off the lights, shuts the drapes, and now it's completely dark. You can't see anything. Then they say to you, "All right, now I want you to rearrange the furniture."

"But I can't see anything," you say to them.

And they say to you, *"Come on! Get motivated! Believe in yourself! You can do it!"*

They're doing what the typical coach or motivational speaker does. They're trying to psych you up by saying that you can do it. Well, that's all well

and good—but you can't see what
the heck you're doing!

Nevertheless, you keep
trying, but you keep hitting
your shins and stubbing your
toes because the room is too
dark for you to see what you're
doing.

MY SUCCESS FORMULA IS 90% INNER GAME, 10% OUTER GAME.

So that coach or motivational speaker starts to
really turn up the heat by saying things like, *"You're
not working hard enough! Hustle! Grind! Winners
never quit and quitters never win!"*

Gee, how are you FEELING right now? Are you
feeling like you want to keep trying to rearrange
furniture that you can't see—or that you'd like to tell
that motivational speaker where he can go?

So here's what I do that's different from those old,
tired methods. I come in to the room you're in, turn
on the light, open the drapes, and let the sunlight in.
Click!

Ah, that's better! Now you can finally SEE
where everything is. Now you can quickly and easily
rearrange the furniture, without working so hard or
struggling—because you can finally see where you
want the furniture to go.

That's what mastering your Inner Game
represents. It's what happens when you realize,

"Wow, I didn't even know that I was holding myself back, or why." That's why so many of my clients say, "This method makes getting what I want so much faster, easier, and far less stressful."

Noah's Note

Some concluding points: It is possible to have a balance (if you want to use that word) of time, energy, relationships and money. That really is happiness; that is success fulfillment. Because if your Focus Factors are out of whack, you're simply not going to be successful, happy or fulfilled. In fact, you'll be stuck, struggling, and unfulfilled—and you won't even know why. You're going to say, "There's something missing, and I don't know what it is." You're at a point of dissatisfaction. That next level is always elusive, always out of reach.

It's right here. We just have to put it in place. You can only do that by understanding what to do and how to do it, having the right plan, the right tools, and the right support so that you can take the right actions. When I'm working with clients, many of them say, "Hey, this isn't as difficult as I thought it would be. Thank God it doesn't have to be so complicated, and it doesn't take very long either!"

It can be pretty quick. As one of my clients put it years ago, "This is like the easy button for success." I like that; I have an easy button on my desk every day to remind me of that. Just keep it simple and say, "That was easy!"

2

Focus Factor 1: Leveraging Your Time

How to Stop Procrastinating and Start Living

You already have all of the Focus Factors that I've described. You have time, even if you don't think you have enough of it. If you're not dead, you have energy. You have relationships, even if they're lousy; you're probably not a hermit living somewhere out in the woods. And you have money, even if you think you don't have enough of that, either. In all of these cases, it's about leveraging: using what you already have to get more of what you want.

That's an empowering concept. Most people start off believing they don't have any of these things; they're in total lack. But you do have something to start with, and it's important to build on that foundation.

At age forty, when I went from basement number one to basement number two, $40,000 in debt, I realized this. I said, "I don't have any money; I don't have what I want; my career hasn't gone the way I wanted." I had just broken up with my girlfriend, so I didn't have any good relationships.

"Wait a minute," I thought. "I'm not dead. I don't have what I want, but I have something. I'm not going to use the excuse of not having. I've got ten fingers and ten

THIS IS WHY "I DON'T HAVE TIME" IS A LIE YOU TELL YOURSELF.

toes. I've got my eyesight. I've got my hearing. I have a lot of things that a lot of people do not have. I have an Internet connection. I have a laptop. I have a brain that works (hopefully). So let's start and build on that."

Similarly, we all have time. You have twenty-four hours in a day. You, me, Bill Gates, Mark Cuban, Richard Branson, Warren Buffett—we all have the same twenty-four hours. When somebody says, "I want to do this, but I don't have the time," they're lying to themselves, although it's a lie they probably believe. You have time, although you may not have made it a priority.

Procrastination: The Thief of Time

One way you waste time is by procrastinating. Procrastination is the most detrimental and unproductive of all habits, because when you are procrastinating, you are stealing from yourself. Procrastination is the thief of time, and as we've seen, time is the one resource we can never get back. The irony of our relationship to time is thinking we're going to live forever. People know that they won't, but they think, "Maybe I will. Maybe I'll be the one."

Maybe you will; who knows? But so far in the game of life, Father Time is undefeated, so probably you're not going to win that one.

Procrastination is one of the habits that I work on the most with my clients. People come to me and say, "Noah, I want to write books like you. I want to have online courses like you've got; I want to be a speaker like you. How do you do it?"

I say, "I do it by doing it. I write books by writing them."

That sounds like a flip answer, but it isn't. Many people say, "I'll get around to it later." When? Why? Ninety-nine out of a hundred times, the answer comes down to fear—fear of getting out of your familiar zone.

Her Book Was in a Shoebox for Fifteen Years—Then I Taught Her This

Years ago I had a client who hired me because she wanted to write a book.

"Great," I said. "Have you started writing your book?"

"Oh, yes."

"Great. Where is it?"

"It's in a shoebox in my closet."

"All right, that's a start," I said. "I'm just curious: how long has it been in a shoebox in your closet?"

"Fifteen years."

I told her, "I see. Well, what if we got it out of the closet? Because right now, your book isn't helping anyone. You have a message. You've obviously got something to say; you've already written it. So why don't we get it out to the world? You can help people. It doesn't matter whether it's fiction or nonfiction. If it's fiction, you're entertaining people. You have a story to tell. If it's nonfiction, you're helping people have more wealth, better health, better relationships—whatever it might be."

Bottom line: I helped her stop procrastinating and get her book out of a shoebox in her closet where it had been sitting for fifteen years. As a result, she published her first book in less than six months.

Time management is a misnomer. We cannot manage time. Time just is. It's going to tick away. Whether we sit and do nothing or are working a hundred hours a week, it does not matter; time doesn't care. That's another myth that I like to bust in this industry: "Time management is so important." That's nice, but you *can't* manage it. Instead, I teach priority management. It comes back to head trash. Say a man wants to make millions

THIS IS WHY TIME MANAGEMENT IS A MYTH.

but puts it off because he has to fix a screen door. Unconsciously, he's saying, "I know I can handle a screen door, but I don't think I can make millions in my business."

I would say to that person, "That's all head trash. Right now, you can't psychologically handle a million dollars in your business, but you can handle a screen door. So why don't we arrange it so that you can handle the million dollars? Maybe you could hire someone to fix the screen door for you." It comes down to priorities.

Find Your Why-To

The number one thing that you can do to overcome procrastination is find your Why-To. Why are you doing X?

Whether you're writing books, creating courses, or putting a video online, you're putting yourself out there to the world. Many people fear: "What if somebody makes fun of me? What if somebody doesn't like my ideas? What if somebody says I look ugly? What if somebody says something bad about me?"

Well, they will.

Your worries and fears along these lines are nothing more than head trash. I still hear head trash every day.

The movie *A Beautiful Mind*, with Russell Crowe, is about a guy who saw things that weren't there, and it got him into a lot of trouble. At the end of the movie, he still saw those things, but he didn't pay any attention to them. That's the way to handle head trash. I still hear the voices: "You can't do it; you're not good enough; you're not smart enough; who do you think you are?" But I don't have to pay any mind to them.

I'm not saying that you'll never hear head trash. I'm giving you strategies so that you can avoid being driven by it. Instead, be driven by a higher purpose— your Why-To.

The word *procrastinate* comes from the Latin word *cras*, which means *tomorrow*. So when you are procrastinating, you are tomorrow-izing. You're saying, "I'll get around to it tomorrow," when you should have done it three months ago. That is a very easy thing to do. That is why time is first here in these Focus Factors of my Freedom Lifestyle Formula. We have to attend to our use of time first, meaning our priorities, because if we don't get those straight, nothing else matters.

Determine What You Want

Now let's look at several of the 7-figure time secrets that will address these issues that we've discussed head-on. Secret number one is, *determine what you want.*

I teach the DBAR cycle. DBAR stands for *desire, belief, action,* and *results.* Everything starts with a desire: what do you want? This affects us at every level, whether it's a matter of wanting a new car, a new house, or a ham sandwich for lunch. We humans are goal-oriented organisms, so understanding what we want is critical for getting what we want. That sounds obvious, but many people come to me and say, "I don't know what I want." I help them to get a sense of clarity about that.

When it comes to desire, there are three different areas to focus on: *having, doing,* and *experiencing.*

I encourage you to write down ten things—possessions—that you want to *have* in the next twelve months. "I want to have a new car." "I want to have a new house." "I want to have X amount coming in from my business per month."

FOCUS ON THESE THREE KEY AREAS OF DESIRE.

Then I want you to list ten things you want to *do* in the next twelve months. What are ten things you want to do? For example: "I want to write a book. I want to create an online course. I want to install a new garage door in my home."

Then I want you to list ten things you want to *experience* in the next twelve months. For instance: "I want to take my family on a Grand Canyon adventure tour. I want to spend two weeks in Hawaii. I want to fly in a hot air balloon." The more specific, the better!

As I stated earlier, the value of things tends to go down over time, whereas the value of experiences goes up. I can still think of my honeymoon and my trip to the Grand Canyon with my wife. I'm sure that you can think of something similar in your life. I encourage you to focus on those experiences. Not that you don't want things—we all want things—but once you get to a certain point, you feel, "I have everything. Everything that I want right now involves what I want to do and experience."

One difficulty is the proliferation of choices. There are many more options today than there were even a few decades ago. You might think that this endless range of choices is great for determining wants, since there's a greater array to match your taste and style, but research shows that it can be debilitating. In his book *The Paradox of Choice*, Barry Schwartz says that at a certain point, a greater number of choices tends to decrease satisfaction. The what-if factor can make it more difficult to determine what you want.

Schwartz talks about the difference between *maximizers* and *satisfiers*. Maximizers have to make sure they've gotten the best out of all possible choices. Satisfiers, as the name suggests, are willing to settle for a choice that they believe is good enough.

This comes down to two basic principles: decision fatigue and FOMO, or the *fear of missing out*. The decision fatigue principle states that we humans can only make so many decisions in a day before the brain quits. When we have too many choices, the brain throws in the towel and says, "Forget it." When we get to the point of decision fatigue, we start to make poor choices.

FOMO, again, is the fear of missing out. That's what maximizers do: "I got this pair of sneakers, but there's a better pair." "I got this car, but there's a better car." Humans are stressed when we have no choices, and also when we have too many choices. Somebody in prison doesn't have any choices, but the rest of us can go online and find ten billion choices. That can be almost as stressful. Not quite the same, but you get the point.

Consequently, we have to narrow our choices down. That's why I start with these three areas: having, doing, and experiencing. That delineation helps people clarify their choices.

Take Your Freedom Temperature

Secret number two is *take your freedom temperature*.
How free do you feel in each of these focused factors
of time, energy, relationships, and money?

Freedom is another way of saying *fulfillment*. We
could easily call this the *7-figure fulfillment formula*,
but I use the word *freedom* simply because most
people don't feel free. If you're in a marriage, you
have made a commitment. That's what a marriage
is: a commitment to this other person, and to the
relationship itself. You're not going to do some
things that you did when you were single. If you
do, you probably won't be married that long. That's
a commitment, but it's a choice that you make each
day. Every relationship requires a commitment.

If you own a business or have a job, you have
commitments as well. You can't just go in, put
your feet on the desk, and say, "Now give me lots
of money." Paying taxes to the government is
something that I also recommend. You probably
should do that.

None of us are free in the total sense of the
word. With freedom comes commitment. Those
two things are inextricably linked. Somebody said
that just as we have a Statue of Liberty on the East
Coast of the United States, we should have a statue of

responsibility on the West Coast, because you cannot have liberty without responsibility.

That much said, most people feel constrained by their current situation: "I don't have the time, energy, relationships, and/or money that I want."

THIS IS HOW TO TAKE YOUR FREEDOM TEMPERATURE.

Taking your freedom temperature is a powerful exercise. Simply take a pencil and paper, and rate yourself on a scale from 1 to 10, with 1 being, "I totally disagree with this statement," and 10 being, "I totally agree with this statement."

1. **Time**. My business and personal life are balanced. My free time is totally free from the business, and I have enough scheduled and protected focus time to work with my best opportunities.

2. **Energy.** I am freed up to work only on what I'm good at and love to do. I'm freed from the things I'm not good at and dislike doing.

3. **Relationships.** In business: I'm leveraged by my team to work only with our best clients and top opportunities. (You can also do a separate reading for personal relationships: I am totally happy in my personal relationships.)

4. **Money.** My company's profitability gives us room to invest in our growth and our team.

Now total up your score. Forty would be the perfect score—all 10s. Nobody scores 40, but what did you get out of a possible 40?

If you scored a 20 or below, we've got an emergency. That means you need to take care of this right away. It's not something you can put off any more.

Next, write down how you are feeling right now. A lot of times when I do this with my clients, they use words like *angry, frustrated, overwhelmed, sad*. They realize, "I am not really free in my life. I didn't know that. I knew I felt something that was off, but I didn't know what it was."

When you look at these Four Focus Factors—time, energy, relationships, money—notice also: did you score higher in one area? Maybe you scored well on one and lower on another. Now we have a great idea of where we need to focus, which is precisely why I call them the Focus Factors.

Freedom From versus Freedom To

Secret three is learning the distinction between *freedom from* and *freedom to*.

Freedom from means being free from certain things that you hate doing. As you know, we humans are motivated by the desire to avoid pain and gain pleasure. What do you want to move away from? What do you want to stop doing? Jim Collins, author of *Good to Great*, says that a "stop doing" list is as important as a to-do list. He's totally right. *Freedom from* involves a stop doing list: "I don't want to do this anymore."

One example: being chained to email. Years ago, that was a big thing for me. I was getting 2,000 emails a day. I spent so much of my day answering them that it was overwhelming. I didn't have anybody to help me. I didn't have the right support system in place.

Finally, I determined that email had to be taken care of, but that didn't mean I had to do it. Think about the owner of a football team, who is, in every case, a billionaire. The owner of the team is not running around throwing the football, getting hit, or getting tackled. He's hiring people to do that. He hires the coaches. He hires the players. He's up there in the box making more money.

We need to think of ourselves like that owner. Something needs to be done, but that doesn't mean I have to do it. Those are two very different things. I came to this realization way too late in my career.

I have a friend who became an entrepreneur at the age of eight, when he started a lawn mowing business. At that young age, he asked his father, "Dad, does having a lawn mowing business mean that I have to mow the lawns?" His father wisely replied, "No, it just means the lawns need to be mowed." So my friend hired other kids to do the mowing. He paid them to do the work, while he managed and marketed the business. Today he's an eight-figure CEO. Smart man!

Unfortunately, it took me longer than it should have to master this element of entrepreneurship. I'm embarrassed to admit that even after I'd been in business for ten years, I was still doing too many things myself and wasn't outsourcing or delegating as I should have been.

If you're an entrepreneur, you must answer this question in order to keep your sanity as well as your freedom: "This is the work that needs to be done, but that does not mean that I have to do it. So who can I hire to get it done on time and under budget?"

EVERY ENTREPRENEUR SHOULD ASK THEMSELVES THIS QUESTION.

In a situation like this, a lot of people think it's a chicken-and-egg situation: "How could I hire someone to help me with this when I don't have the money? But if I don't get it done, then I'm not going to have any money."

Then get it as fast as you can. If you have a Why-To that's strong enough, you find the way. That's what I did. I didn't have enough money either, but I found the money because I found the why. When you find the why, you find the way.

Social media is another major time suck for many people. One of the biggest problems with social media is that if you want more impact, influence, and income, you need to do it—however, it can also suck hours from your day that you could be using on more profitable activities.

Make a list of ten things you want freedom from. For example, you might write: "*I want freedom from doing email every day. I want freedom from managing my social media. I want freedom from bookkeeping or managing client files.*" Those are just a few examples of things you might want freedom from doing.

A lot of entrepreneurs, especially the ones who are having trouble getting to the next level, have trouble delegating. You may say, "But Noah, I don't have anybody to delegate to." No kidding, but we've got to start where we are. You have what you have. You have the time, energy, relationships, and money you have. Rather than sitting there, dreaming, hoping, and wishing, let's boil it down. Let's get focused, take a deep breath, and then we can move forward: "I want to stop doing these things; I want to get them off my plate."

Freedom to refers to the things that you want to be doing in your life. This list represents the opposite of your *freedom from* list, because your *freedom to* list includes activities you want to have the time to do that you probably aren't doing right now.

Freedom from and *freedom to* are two sides of the same coin. As I stated earlier, we all have the same twenty-four hours in a day. That means that you're probably doing some things in your business that you'd rather not be doing, but that need to be done nevertheless. Conversely, perhaps you're not doing certain things that you'd really love to be doing.

Therefore, list ten things you want freedom from (e.g., being chained to email, social media, trying to figure everything out yourself, etc.) and ten things you want the freedom to do (e.g., invest in new technologies, learn new things, participate in mastermind groups, create and innovate, etc.).

Once you have both of these lists, you'll have a roadmap of where you want to be in the next twelve months, so you can implement a plan of action to get there!

The Belief Gap

Secret number four has to do with the real reason you're stuck: *your belief gap*. This is another way of talking about your head trash.

Look at where you are right now. That's what I call your *current perceived reality* or your CPR. It's where you think you are right now. You have what you have. You have the time, the energy, relationships, and money that you have, and that's where you are. That's your current perceived reality.

Notice I said *perceived* reality. When I was $40,000 in debt and working out of my parents' basement at the age of forty, I was there because that's where I thought I should be or would be (as crazy as that sounds). Even after all that work on myself, I still had so much head trash.

Your CPR is where you are. Picture yourself standing on cliff, with a chasm in front of you. Beyond it is another cliff with your *new desired reality*: your NDR. That's your pot of gold at the end of the rainbow. That's where you have the time, energy, relationships, and money that you want.

So here you are in your CPR, and you're looking at your NDR, but you just can't get there. What is standing between you and where you want to be?

THIS IS HOW TO GO FROM WHERE YOU ARE TO WHERE YOU WANT TO BE.

It really comes down to your belief gap. Your belief gap is that part of you that says, "I want to have this, but I probably can't do it because . . ."

Did you know that whatever comes after the word *because* is what you firmly believe and will defend to the death? Isn't it ironic how much we humans will fight for our limitations? We do this because our limitations make us feel safe. However, as Stephen Covey, author of *The Seven Habits of Highly Successful People*, said, "When you defend your limitations, you get to keep them." That's one of the man reasons you need to stop defending your limitations.

Will Rogers said, "It ain't what a man don't know that gets him in trouble; it's what he knows that ain't so." It's not what we don't know that keeps us stuck; it's what we believe that isn't true. But if we believe it, we make it true.

How long does it take to acquire a new belief? When you use my Afformations Method, you can change your beliefs very quickly. In fact, I invented Afformations because I was so frustrated by the fact that I'd been using the old affirmations technique for so many years and never saw results.

While the old affirmation technique helped many people change their beliefs, there are also countless cases where the old technique *didn't* work that we rarely hear about. Interestingly, one place where people feel safe to admit that the old technique didn't work for them is my seminars. That's because, as The Father of Afformations, people feel safe to tell me that, just like me, they tried the old "affirmation" technique and it really didn't work for them, either. That's why a big part of my mission is to create a safe environment for people to tell the truth about who they really are and what actually works (and doesn't work) for them.

That's why I'm saying it here: I did affirmations, and they didn't work for me. So I invented something better, based on how the brain actually works, which is with questions. You are asking questions every second of every day, whether you know it or not. You're sowing seeds of thought. If you're sowing lousy thought seeds, which say, "I can't do it because..." there you are. There is your life. You sowed those seeds. Of course you didn't mean to; nobody does it on purpose. Nobody wakes up in the morning and says, "Wow, this is a beautiful day. The birds are singing. The sun is shining. I think I'll hold myself back from success today."

Nobody says that consciously. My Inner Game work has to do with the subconscious mind. We're bringing the subconscious to the conscious. Again, it's like turning on a light in a room that's dark. That dark room is your subconscious.

Strivers and the Just Fine

In the four decades that I've been coaching, I've noticed that there are two basic kinds of people: the strivers, who want more, and the people who are just fine. If you're just fine, you're probably not reading this book right now. Since you are reading it, you're probably a striver, and you're saying, "I do want more. I've tried a whole bunch of things, but I'm still not where I want to be."

If you're feeling fine where you are, I'm happy for you. I am not here to tell you what you should or should not want. I'm rare in this industry, because most motivational speakers say you've always got to be striving. If you're happy and comfortable, more power to you. The only people who come to me are those that are striving, and ninety-nine times out of a hundred, they've tried lots of different things that haven't worked.

Twelve Months from Now

Let's move on to secret number five. Imagine that you have worked with me as a coach for the last twelve months. Ask yourself, what would have happened in your life for you to feel happy with your progress? Get a very clear picture, going back to your desires to have, do, and experience. What does your pot of gold look like?

THIS IS WHAT HAPPENS WHEN YOU ARGUE FOR YOUR LIMITATIONS.

Now that you have a clear picture of what you want, ask, why don't you have it yet? What is standing in your way or holding you back?

I hope that you have a better picture of this now. You're hopefully realizing, "My head trash is holding me back. It's a belief that I don't have enough time, energy, relationships, or money. It's me telling myself that I can't be happy and rich. It's me telling myself that my spouse won't let me do it," or whatever the excuse might be.

Remember, the more you fight for your limitations, the more you get to keep them. Would you rather be right or rich? Would you rather be right or happy? It's ironic that most people would rather be right than happy or rich.

However, you're not most people, are you? That's why you're reading this book right now. Therefore, start to open the door to new possibilities right now—and realize that you can be happy, spiritual and rich all at the same time!

The Hidden Cost of Head Trash

Secret number six: *ask yourself, how much is your head trash costing you*? If you don't take out your head trash, it's costing you right now. I have never worked with a client who didn't tell me that their head trash was costing them at least $10,000 a month. That's a lot of money.

Therefore, answer these questions so you can stop losing out on the wealth and opportunity that's right in front of you:

1. How do you see your head trash holding you back right now? How is it holding you back in time, energy, relationships, and money?

2. What will it cost you if you don't get rid of your head trash about money, wealth, relationships, and time? If you just keep doing what you're doing, what's it going to cost you?

3. Would you rather dump your head trash sooner or later? Do you want to get around to it later? How about now?

This exercise is all about finding your Why-To.

Money Reveals Everything

Money doesn't change anything, but it reveals everything. Money is like a magnifying glass. If you are a jerk without any money and all of a sudden you get money, you'll just be a rich jerk. But if you are a thoughtful and generous person and you get money, you'll be more thoughtful and generous. You'll have more ability to help others and serve your community.

People have asked me many times, "If I make a lot of money, is that going to ruin my relationships? Is it going to fix my relationships?"

I say, yes, it'll do both. It's going to ruin some, and it's going to fix others. First of all, if you make a lot of money, lots of relatives that you didn't even know you had will be holding their hands out. For example, many professional athletes came from struggling backgrounds, and all of a sudden, they're millionaires. Often they're very young, in their early twenties, and all these friends and cousins that they didn't even know they had will be holding their hands out. That's really tough, because the athletes want to help. They want to give back to

THIS IS WHY SO MANY MILLIONAIRE ATHLETES GO BROKE.

the community and their friends. That's why so many professional athletes end up broke after making tens of millions of dollars.

As great as it is that you want to help, when you give handouts to people who haven't earned it, they simply feel inclined to keep asking for more. You think that if you help the person, they will start to help themselves. It doesn't work that way. They actually become more dependent on you.

That's why one of the habits in my Power Habits® System is to *Claim Your Power*—finding the inner strength to stop letting people become dependent on you. For example, many highly successful people find it very difficult to say no to people they love. However, many of my clients have come to realize that just because someone is related to you, doesn't mean they have your best interests at heart.

Where Are You Playing Small?

Secret number seven is, *find where you are playing small*. For this exercise, I want you to answer the following questions:

1. Where are you playing small? Are you playing small in your life, your health, your relationships, your business, your impact, your influence? In

what areas are you holding yourself back right now?

2. What are the costs to you of playing small?

3. What are the costs to others of your playing small? You may think that it really doesn't affect anyone else, but it does. So what is the pain to others?

4. What is the cost of indecision in your life? Napoleon Hill said that the leaders in every walk of life decide quickly and firmly, so when you decide quickly and firmly, you get to be a leader. That doesn't mean you're going to be right all the time, but at least you're failing forward rather than sitting there thinking, "I hope I win the lottery."

5. Why does your impact matter? Most people say, "It doesn't really matter what I do." Maybe it doesn't in the grand scheme of things, but we all can and do have an effect on people. If you're holding yourself back, if you're playing small, you will not have the impact, influence, or income that you want.

Answer these questions to identify the areas in your life that you are playing small right now. Did you realize that when you play small, it affects other people as well as yourself? For example, if I had not written my books and created my online courses like *Permission to Succeed*®, *The Afformations*® *Advantage* and *Power Habits*® *Academy*, more than a million people would not have had their lives changed through my work.

This is not an exercise in self-aggrandizement; it's an exercise to help you understand the impact you have and can have on others and on this planet. Ironically, while some people are motivated by money and status, others are more motivated by the impact they have on others.

That's why I want you to do this exercise—to help you understand what actually motivates you, what your impact is and can be, and why you playing small doesn't help anybody.

Activities versus Outcomes

Secret number eight is to *focus on activities rather than outcomes.*

Many personal development experts suggest that you can control outcomes. There are scores of programs that have you visualize the result and not worry about the process for getting there; just visualize the result and it'll magically happen. What planet are they on? I've never seen that happen.

Ninety-nine percent of the time, you have to make it happen.

That is the difference between activities and outcomes. The problem is, you can't actually control outcomes. Here's an example. There are thirty-two teams in the National Football League, and every single one of them wants to win the Super Bowl. Every year, thirty-two teams say, "We want to win the Super Bowl." There are fifty-three players on each team, plus the coaching staff, trainers, team doctors, and so on; every one of whom is focused on obtaining this single outcome every year: winning the Super Bowl. But each year, thirty-one of those teams do *not* win the Super Bowl. Does that mean they're a bunch of losers? No, of course not. It means you can't control the outcome.

Bill Walsh, the legendary coach of the San Francisco 49ers, in his book *The Score Takes Care of Itself* wrote that in football, when you focus on the little things, the big things tend to take care of themselves. For example, Coach Walsh famously scripted the first twenty-five plays of every game and in practice, helped his players focus on tiny details like arm position when throwing the ball and feet movement when blocking.

In fact, he taught the opposite of those who tell you to just visualize the outcome and it'll take care of itself, because that's not how it works. Coach Walsh—one of the greatest coaches in any sport—taught that while you can control what you do in any situation, you simply can't control what's going to happen as a result of any particular play.

For example, when I watch football, I often joke that the team with the ball should call a touchdown. In other words, every player on every team would like every play to result in a touchdown. Of course, that's not how it works in real life. Some plays result in a positive gain, some plays result in a negative loss, and some end up right in the same spot as before. Great coaches teach that while we can't control outcomes, we CAN control how we respond to any given situation.

There are only three things that we humans can control: what we think, what we say, and what we do. That's it. We can control our thoughts, our words, and our actions.

THESE ARE THE ONLY THREE THINGS WE CAN CONTROL.

Here's an exercise along these lines. For the next seven days, write down every instance where you catch yourself trying to control an outcome—in football terms, calling a touchdown—versus focusing on what you can do about it: calling the play. Then use this guide to help you get your focus back to where it needs to be.

Here are some questions that I encourage you to ask, to help you stay focused on what you can control, rather than worrying about things that are out of your control:

1. What outcome do I want here?
2. What are the obstacles in my way of achieving that outcome?
3. What am I doing right now to try and control the outcome?
4. What can I do to *influence* the outcome, rather than trying to control it?

The Entrepreneurial Yellow Brick Road

I talk about the yellow brick road of entrepreneurial success. The yellow brick road has certain milestones on it: making your first $10,000, your first $100,000, your first $1 million. But you have to lay the bricks along the way. You can say, "I want $1 million." It's fine that you want that, but that's an outcome. But you can lay the bricks, asking, "What am I doing today to get to that outcome?"

Entrepreneurs tend to be intensely focused on outcomes, and they're looking at the numbers every month. The numbers are very important. Without profit, you're not in business. The problem is that the numbers are a lagging indicator: they're a result of something else. Leading indicators, by contrast, are the things that cause the lagging indicators, mainly money.

For example, in order to move to your next milestone along the entrepreneurial yellow brick road—whether it's your next $10,000, your next $100,000 or your next million—you need to focus on the three pillars of growing your business: increasing the number of customers; increasing the number of purchases that each customer makes; and increasing the amount of profit you make from each customer purchase.

Why are these so crucial? Because these are all leading indicators. Here are some critical questions you need to ask in order to focus on these leading indicators:

1. How much does it cost me to get a customer right now (cost per acquisition, or CPA)?

2. What is the lifetime value of a customer (LTV) to my business?

3. How am I attracting customers right now? For example: social media, SEO (search engine optimization), paid ads, referrals, affiliates, etc.

4. What can I do to increase the value that I'm giving my customers so they spend more with me?

5. How can I add even more value to my customers so they buy more frequently from me?

When you consistently ask these questions and focus on these leading indicators, it will create a cycle of success that will lead you down the yellow brick road to success.

FOCUS ON LEADING INDICATORS TO DRIVE YOUR SUCCESS.

Afformations on Time

Let me conclude with some specific Afformations related to the topic of this chapter.

To refresh your memory: Afformations are empowering questions that change your subconscious thought patterns from negative to positive, using the embedded presupposition factor of the brain.

Remember that, like every single person on this planet, you're already using Afformations. The problem is, most people are doing it in a negative, disempowering way. Furthermore, most people don't know they're doing it at all. That's why my mission is to help raise the consciousness of humanity, one question at a time.

Here are my top ten Afformations for this Focus Factor of Time Freedom:

1. Why do I leverage my time so well?

2. Why do I stop doing the things I want freedom from?

3. Why do I get paid for doing what I'm great at?

4. Why do I delegate activities that aren't highly profitable?

5. Why do I have all the time I need to do the things I really want to do?

6. Why do I treat my time as my most precious asset?

7. Why do I start getting paid for being who I really am?

8. Why do I stop trying to control outcomes?

9. Why am I focused on what I can do every day to get the things I really want?

10. Why am I always in the right place at the right time, doing the right things with the right people?

By the way, you can get audios of my 101 favorite Afformations at **iAfform.com.** You can listen to them to reprogram your subconscious thought patterns even while you're not paying attention.

Noah's Note

To sum up: you cannot control time; you can only control your actions. There is no such thing as time management; there's only priority management and action management. Take control of your thoughts, words, and actions, and that will change your life and your relationship to time—the most valuable resource we have.

3

Focus Factor 2: Leverage Your Energy

How to Tap Your Four Resources of Daily Energy

Energy is crucial. If you don't have energy, you're not alive. Moreover, the types of energy are important, yet most people aren't aware of them, which is one reason why they feel distracted. This is one of the things that people write to me about most often: "Noah, I've got too many things going on. I'm distracted all the time; I can't focus." Living in a world of infinite distractions, most people haven't been taught how to manage their energy.

Often when people think of high energy, they imagine a person who's up early, who's extroverted, charismatic. You can feel their energy when you're around them. They're juggling multiple projects, and they're still able to tend to all of their key relationships.

Energy is more complex than that. I am an introvert, which most people wouldn't believe when they hear me: "But Noah, you've got so much energy." That's because I've learned how to manage my sources of energy. I'm different when I'm on stage, because if I talked like someone with little energy, people would be falling asleep. But if I'm at a party, I'm not the guy dancing around with a lampshade on his head. I'd rather talk to one person at a time and just be.

The Four Types of Energy

We need to know the four different types of energy so that we can manage and focus them. They are:

1. Physical
2. Emotional
3. Mental
4. Spiritual

Physical energy has to do with the body. My wife's a great example; she's got a ton of physical energy. We can't keep up with her; she has kids in their twenties and thirties who can't keep up with her. She runs circles around everybody.

This is what most people think of when they hear the word *energy*. But there are three other types as well. All of them work together to create a whole person.

The second type is emotional. If physical energy has to do with the *quantity* of energy you have, emotional energy has to do with the *quality*. These two are closely connected. It's relatively unlikely that if you are a high-energy person physically, you will also be depressed all the time. Similarly, someone who's emotionally depressed will tend to have little physical energy.

As a result, you can changing one by changing the other. On an extremely simple level, you can improve your mood by getting up and walking around. When you assume a power pose, standing the way a confident person would stand, you feel more confident.

THIS IS WHY LEVERAGING YOUR ENERGY IS SO IMPORTANT.

Mental energy is your ability to focus. That's hugely important because of the infinite number of distractions that we live with every day.

Spiritual energy is your sense of purpose or connection to something larger than yourself. Emerson said that the greatest happiness lies within you when you are connected to a purpose greater than yourself.

I think we've all met people like that. Steve Jobs was great at this. He once said he wanted to teach machines to think like humans rather than trying to make humans think like machines. Of course there are numerous other examples: Mahatma Gandhi, Martin Luther King Jr. When John F. Kennedy talked about going to the moon, he said that we don't do these things because they're easy. We do them because they're hard.

You know how you sometimes feel tired, frustrated, stressed out, and overwhelmed? How you can be working all day, yet at the end of the day, feel like nothing got done? One reason is because no one's taught you how to manage your sources of energy.

For example, if you don't manage your physical energy, you might tire easily and can't do the things you really want to do. If you don't manage your emotional energy, you'll probably feel depressed, frustrated, angry, or resentful. If you don't manage your mental energy, you'll find it very difficult to focus and make important decisions. You'll also have difficulty taking action or following through on plans, which means you'll have difficulty setting and achieving your goals.

Finally, if you don't have a sense of purpose, you could find yourself saying, "I've made lots of money. Now what do I do?" Money is a great tool, but in itself it's not enough. My whole teaching is about looking at the entirety of the human being and understanding how to master it to reach your goals and be happy as you're doing it.

Spending and Renewing

There are two things we can do with our energy: spend it and renew it. It is very much like the battery in your phone. If you keep using your phone all the time without recharging it, it goes dead. It's the same thing with us human beings. All of these types of energy have to be renewed. Unfortunately, we're not trained in how to do it. You didn't take a class in high school about renewing your energy. That's why I love the personal growth industry: it fills in the gaps in our knowledge left by our education. Renewing our energy is not that hard; we just have to train ourselves.

Most people can tell when they're physically exhausted and depleted; your body tells you that you're at a low ebb, you need renewal. But they neglect the other three forms of energy until they're at a crisis point. In fact, I would argue that the spiritual aspect of purpose—finding your Why-To—is both the most important and the one that we neglect the most.

How to Take Your Energy Inventory

Let's begin by taking an energy inventory. Rate yourself from one to ten on your level of energy in these four areas—physical, emotional, mental, and spiritual. One would mean that you have very low energy in this area, while ten would be very high energy.

My wife, for example, would be a ten on the physical and emotional levels. Mentally, it would be less: she's not that great at focusing; she gets distracted easily, and she'll be the first to tell you that. Spiritually, she's probably a ten, because she's very connected to a larger purpose.

Once you have rated yourself in each of the four areas, ask, what is your highest rated energy source right now? Why do you feel that is the case? I personally would be a tie between mental and spiritual. I'm very able to focus my mental energy, and my spiritual purpose energy level is also very high. The physical and emotional levels are lower, although they're still good.

Next, what is your lowest rated form of energy right now? Why?

For me, it would be physical. I don't really like exercising, but I know the benefits of exercising, so I do it.

Practical Tips for Energy Building

Now that you have an awareness of where your energy reserves are strong and where they're weak, let's start with some practical tips in each area. Let's begin with the physical. The three keys to renewing your physical energy are:

1. Proper eating
2. Proper exercise
3. Proper sleep

These three prongs of the trident, if you will, are the keys to renewing your physical energy.

Let's start with food. Food is the fuel that you put in your body. So if you put the wrong fuel in even the best car, you've got a car that won't run. Neither will you as a human being.

I suggest that for the next seven days, you list everything that you eat and rate it from one to ten. One means it's really bad for you. Ten is, it's good for you. We all know what those things are. It's very simple. If God made it, it's good. If it's manmade, it's bad.

Look in your kitchen right now. What foods do you have? Are they manmade or are they God-made? By God-made, I mean, fruits, vegetables, meats, and dairy. We humans can't create a chicken; we can't create broccoli. God made those things. That's why we've been eating them for millennia. But man came along and decide to make processed food. Ninety-nine times out of a hundred, manmade foods are going to rob you of energy.

THIS IS THE SIMPLEST METHOD TO EAT HEALTHIER.

In any grocery store in the United States, all you have to do is shop on the outside of the aisles. What is on the outside? Produce, meats, fruits and vegetables, dairy. The inside aisles are taken up with manmade carbs: chips, cookies, brownies, bread, pasta. Is it all bad? Pretty much.

I'm not saying this as a judgment. We're just looking at energy. I don't want you to judge yourself if you say, "Oh my gosh! All I eat is manmade junk." Probably true, because if you're in the United States, that's what you've been inundated with. That is the point of this exercise, to make you realize, "Gosh, I didn't even know."

After you've done this for seven days, list the foods that you can stop eating because they are robbing you of energy.

Exercise

Let's turn now to exercise. The human body was designed to move, not sit and stare at a computer all day long, and yet that's exactly what so many of us do. There may be and will be long periods of time when that's exactly what you have to do as a modern-day entrepreneur. That's why it's essential to practice healthy movement habits every day.

Here's what you can do to start to leverage your physical energy in the area of exercise. Begin by listing three free and simple ways you can move your body every day.

For example, you could stand up and walk around your home. If you're ambitious, walk around the block. You do not have to join a gym. You do not have to pay a lot of money. I've tried joining a gym four different times in my life and hated it every time.

THIS IS HOW TO BEAT THE "I DON'T HAVE TIME TO EXERCISE" EXCUSE.

Each day at work, set a timer for ninety minutes. When it goes off, get up from your desk and move your body, even if it's just going for a walk around your home or office.

For the first week, commit yourself to doing ten minutes of exercise each day. You don't have to spend hours at the gym if you don't want to. You can, of course, but you don't have to. That's another form of head trash: "If I have to exercise, I've got to join a gym, and I don't have the time." No, you do not. Notice that I'm taking away your excuses not to exercise.

Next, list three reasons why you want to exercise. I know my Why-To: I want to live. I want to be happy. I don't want to be overweight. I want to feel good in my old age; I want to be able to get around.

My father is in his eighties, and he's a spry old guy. He visited us recently at our three-story house, and he was going up and down the stairs like nothing. Maybe he's not jogging around the block, yet he's still a very active person well into his eighties. That's what I want to be.

I have done a lot of research on exercise, and ten minutes a day is all you need. Most Americans get zero, so anything more than zero is something. Again, I'm is taking away your excuses: "I can't do it because I don't have the time." Really? A week has 168 hours in it. You don't have ten minutes a day to change your life? I guess you don't want it that much.

Of course, there are many ways to exercise. Work with your own body, and listen to it. I prefer to exercise in the morning, before breakfast, on an empty stomach. I do low-impact aerobic exercises, and I vary them so I don't get bored.

There are programs you could use. You could go on YouTube and type in "ten-minute exercise." They're all free. You don't have the money? There's no money involved, or at any rate there doesn't have to be.

That's the point: I want you to start catching yourself when you're making these excuses: "I can't do it because . . ." There is no *because* here.

Sleep

The next area of self-care is sleep. Sleep is a subject that wasn't discussed very much even ten or fifteen years ago. People even made it a point of pride to say that they'd only gotten three hours of sleep. If you were sleeping too much, you were a loser. A lot of people still believe that—the "hustle and grind" crowd. Personally, I want to live. I want to be happy. I don't care about having a billion dollars if I'm miserable.

Sleep is crucial to your health, happiness, and well-being, as well as your physical, emotional, mental, and spiritual energy. Everybody is different, so listen to your body. Some people are morning people. Some people are evening people. Some are night owls. Some are early birds. I like to get up at about seven o'clock every morning, but sometimes I'm up at four because I'll get an idea, and I'll take the seventeen-second commute from my bedroom to my office, write some notes on my computer, and go right back to bed.

By the way, it's not just the quantity of sleep that you get that's important, but the quality—true, deep sleep, when you're dreaming—REM sleep.

To ensure quality sleep, you want to have the same routine at night, every night. You've got to have a set time when you're telling your body it's time for bed.

Next, dim the lights in your home. We humans are on a circadian rhythm. We respond to sunlight, but with electricity, we now have a lot of nonnatural light in our homes. Many people leave the lights on all the time. Your body is asking, "What am I supposed to do here? Are we awake? Are we sleeping?" You have to actually dim the lights.

Number three is, don't watch television for at least an hour before going to bed. That's ideal, but at least turn the television off for a minimum of a half hour beforehand.

You could also take a bath or a Jacuzzi. That's a nice way to relax. Also relaxing music or white noise. My website iAfform.com has an audio called "Deep Blissful Sleep." It has 101 Afformations to help you sleep better.

Leverage Your Emotional Energy

Your emotional life is determined by your opinion of your past, your present, and your future. Years ago, I realized that a person's emotional life could be summed up in just two sentences: When your opinion of your past, present, and future tends to be positive, you will be happy. When your opinion of your past, present, or future tends to be negative, you will be unhappy. That is your entire emotional life.

YOUR EMOTIONAL LIFE CAN BE SUMMED UP IN THESE TWO SENTENCES.

The key word in those two sentences is *opinion*. It is not what happens to us, but our opinion of what happens to us. That is what creates our emotional life. Consequently, to leverage your emotional energy, you only need to do three things:

1. Forgive your past.
2. Appreciate your present.
3. Step into your best future.

I truly believe that these three things—forgiveness, gratitude, and confidence—cover everything.

Forgiveness can take a long time. It can be difficult. What I have noticed, both in myself and in my clients, is that the hardest person to forgive is ourselves.

For this stage, make a list: Whom do I need to forgive? For what and why? Why did I choose to forgive them? Forgiveness is a choice, and you can choose to forgive or not forgive. When I do this exercise, there's nobody really left for me to forgive except myself.

In those ten years from 1997 to 2007, I paid all those "gurus" lots of money, but they took me down a bad path and got me into worse shape than when I started. I can sit here and blame them. For years I did, but then I said, "Well, Noah, who was the person who hired them?" That was me. Then I beat myself up: "What an idiot! I can't believe I was so dumb and listened to those clowns." It's easy to get into a process of self-flagellation.

Most people you meet have gone through traumatic events. Some may even say, "How can I forgive that person for what they did to me?" However, when you forgive someone, you're not condoning bad behavior or "letting them off the hook" as some believe. The fact is, it's nearly impossible to reach a certain age without having had a number of traumatic, hurtful things happen to you.

That's why I believe that forgiveness is something we must do every day, like bathing. In fact, just as we need to cleanse our physical bodies daily, we also need to cleanse our metaphysical bodies every day through the process of forgiveness.

That's why we have to take out the trash in our homes every day: because trash will accumulate, whether we like it or are consciously aware of it or not. Now just imagine how many people you know who haven't taken out the trash in their HEAD for years or even decades! That's why we must also follow this method to take out the head trash that can hold us back without our conscious awareness.

Think about that term *head trash*. What is trash? Trash happens throughout life. As you're eating, you create trash. It just accumulates through the process of life. Imagine your home, and imagine saying, "You know what? I don't think I want to take out the trash this week." You let it pile up for the week. The next week goes by, and you don't feel like taking it out then either. You let it pile up for a month. A year goes by, maybe five or ten years, and you still haven't taken out the trash. What does your home look like now? Pretty bad. That's why

THIS IS WHY IT'S CRUCIAL TO TAKE OUT YOUR HEAD TRASH.

we have to take out the trash every day: because it's just going to accumulate, whether we're aware of it or not. Imagine how many people you know who haven't taken out the trash in their heads for decades.

The Power of Gratitude

Regarding the second piece: gratitude. This is easy to do when things are going well in your life, but difficult when you're in the midst of turmoil. When I was at my low point in 2007, I said, "Noah, what are you going to do?" I decided to practice this process: forgive my past, appreciate my present, and somehow step into my best future. I asked, what do I have to be grateful for? Let's see:

- You've got ten fingers.
- You've got ten toes.
- You've got eyes that see.
- You've got ears that hear.

- You've got a brain that thinks.
- You have an Internet connection.
- You have a laptop.
- Your muscles work.
- You can walk.
- You can talk.
- You can think.
- You can listen.
- You can learn.

Millions of people don't have at least some of those things. I'm not saying I'm better or worse than anyone. I'm just saying, this is what I have. Thank God I have these things.

I believe that gratitude is the king of all positive emotion. It's a process, and a conscious one. Because I came from a depressed family, I am not prone to gratitude; I'm prone to look at everything that's wrong. That's my natural thought, which I've had to fight: "No, I'm going to be grateful right now. I don't have everything that I want, but who does? What do I have?"

This goes back to the point of leverage: using what you have to get what you want. I have these things; what am I going to do? That's when I hired the business coach who helped me turn my life around. He was the first person to believe in me and give me a strategy for getting out of that bad situation. That's what I'm now privileged to be able to do for my clients.

How to Increase Your Confidence

Some people believe that you are either blessed with confidence or you're not.

I never considered myself a high-confidence person. In high school, I was a nerd before it was cool to be a nerd. I was far from cool. I had Coke bottle glasses, a face full of acne, a big Afro, and zero self-confidence. I would walk around school, and I wouldn't look people in the eye; I would be hunched over. I didn't have any confidence at all.

I was, however, very much into the arts. I was an art nerd along with being a Latin nerd and all the other nerds you could be. I would be in plays and musicals, which got me out of my shell, because I was performing. But when I went back to real life, I would go back to being shy.

Confidence is a muscle. It is a skill that you can develop. It took me years and years to develop that skill. One of the things that was hardest for me was saying what was on my mind, because I would just

CONFIDENCE IS A MUSCLE YOU CAN DEVELOP.

go along with people. Finally I said, "I'm going to start speaking up for myself, even if I'm wrong. Who cares? Nobody's right all the time, right?" At least talk. At least open your mouth. People can't read your mind. They don't know what's in your head if you don't tell them.

Now I often ask for things that I feel I have no chance of getting. Nine times out of ten, I get them. I will ask just because I feel like it, and now it's more like a game.

By the way, the word *confidence* comes from the Latin *confidere*, which means *to trust in, to trust within*. Trust within yourself. Most people do not have that sense of self-confidence, especially us introverts, and we tend to let the extroverts run roughshod over us. So my advice to all introverts is, speak up.

Leverage Your Mental Energy

Mental energy has to do with focus, which is absolutely critical. As I've said, 90 percent of the people who write to me now tell me that their number one issue is focus.

As a matter of fact, I am naturally good at focus. It's a strong muscle for me and always has been. But that doesn't mean I can't teach it. So I started to break down what I do in order to focus, and now I'm able to teach it to others.

Most people just go on working, working, working, and they never take a break. They never stop. And they wonder, why is my mind wandering? Why can't I focus?

THIS IS WHY LACK OF FOCUS KEEPS SO MANY PEOPLE STUCK.

It's because scientific studies have shown that human beings work best in ninety-minute sprints. After that, our attention and ability to focus decrease very sharply.

No doubt you get up in the morning, and you're excited and raring to go. Then the energy starts dropping, and you're wondering what happened. Actually, nothing. You're not doing anything wrong. You're a human being, so you've got to recharge your battery. Rather than fighting human nature, which does not work, start using it to your advantage so that you can get more of the results that you want.

Set a timer, and do ninety minutes of focused work. Your body will tell you. I have this down to a science so much now that after I've been working for ninety minutes, I get up almost to the minute. I never look at my timer anymore. I just think, "I'm feeling a little tired right now. I feel like I need a little stretch." This too is a muscle you can develop.

Ten to fifteen minutes is a good time for a break. Of course, there will be things you have to get done at a certain time, so you may have to rearrange your schedule to attend to them first. But especially when we're working from home, many tasks have no fixed deadline: they can be done whenever. That's where we go back to procrastination.

Ten to fifteen minutes is generally enough, so if you feel like taking a nap, take one. Listen to your body. Your body will tell you. People say, "If I listen to my body, I'll just sleep all day." Well, then, sleep all day; take a day off; take a mental health day. We all need those. Give yourself permission to take time off.

Here are some questions to help you in this area of focus.

1. Write down the top three outcomes that you want to achieve this week. Here I am talking about outcomes, because we're focusing on what we want, our desires. What do you want to achieve? I said three things. You may be thinking, "But I've got fifty things to do." This is one problem: you're trying to do too much, so stop and narrow it down to top three.

2. Write down which outcome has the highest probable rate of return. It means that if I do or get this one thing, it's going to make a huge difference for me in my business, health, money, relationships—whatever it might be. Of course,

we can never know to the tenth decimal place, but we can take a good guess.

3. What is the next action for completing this outcome? Now we're focused on what we can do: activities versus outcome. What's the very next thing that I can do? Write an email? Make a phone call? Do research on the web? Talk to a friend? Whatever it might be, there's always one next thing that you can do. You're laying that next brick, and you have control of that.

4. What resources do I have to help me get what I want? You have time, energy, relationships, and money. "Oh, but I don't have what I need." OK, what do you have?

5. What resources do I need? There are resources you have and resources you need. You can think, you can talk, you can pick up the phone, you can do research on the Internet; again, there's always something you can do. You can do it. You have the power. That's why it's called empowerment. You have the power, but you've got to know that you do.

6. Who can help me get what I need and what am I willing to give in return? If you say, "I don't have the time; I don't have the money," your Why-To is not strong enough. When you can find the why, you can find the way.

Leverage Your Spiritual Energy

Your spiritual energy is your connection to your purpose on the earth. I call this *finding your because*. The more connected you are to your purpose or mission, the more energy you have to move through the setbacks and reversals that life throws at you. Things don't always go your way, and setbacks are a part of life, especially when your *because* is very big. When you have a great purpose, sometimes you have great reversals. That happens very frequently.

If you don't know your purpose, when things get hard, you'll quit. But if you have a greater purpose, even when reversals happen, you know that they're just another part of the journey. They're something that you'll talk about and hopefully laugh about later.

Today it's all about the superficial—the now, the hot, the cool. But when you are focused on the superficial, you are not focused on the deep. They are at odds with each other. Say your purpose is helping kids, helping education, or helping veterans. (These are topics that are very important to me personally.) When you think, "I've got to make money today," you'll have that level of energy. But if you're thinking about how it's because you want to help veterans, that raises your energy instantly. I see this across the board both when I work on myself and when I work with my clients. When you're focused on the fact that you need to make money, your energy goes down. There's nothing wrong with needing or wanting or getting money. We all have to have it in order to live on this planet. Yet it's a very low frequency of energy.

Conversely, it raises your energy when you talk about wanting to help people, but it can't just be in a general sense: "I want to help people." That doesn't really mean anything. But when I talk specifically about helping veterans and their families, it raises my energy, because that's a very important topic to me. Veterans have sacrificed so much, yet they have been terribly underserved, especially in the area of mental health, happiness, and fulfillment. So that is a mission for me. Even thinking about it, talking about it, knowing that I'm moving towards that every day, makes me know that I'm connected to something larger than a need to make money.

This is very multilayered approach. That's why we call it the 7-Figure Freedom Lifestyle. It is a lifestyle that is

THIS IS WHY THE 7-FIGURE LIFE IS A MULTI-LAYERED APPROACH.

three-dimensional. Money is great, but that's just one part of it. When we look at the whole person, that's when you become a whole person, and happiness evolves naturally. You become happy because you're serving a larger purpose. In his classic book *Man's Search for Meaning*, Viktor Frankl said that when you pursue happiness, happiness goes away, but when you pursue meaning, happiness ensues.

Your Perfect Average Day

As for determining your purpose, there are many ways to do that. You could argue that every religion is based upon the question of what our purpose is here on earth, so certainly I will not be able to give a cohesive and all-encompassing vision of purpose.

Nevertheless, one way I help my clients get started is to encourage them to write a vision of their perfect average day. For instance, if you were living your perfect average day, what would it look like? What would you be doing if you were living your perfect average day? What do you get to do? Not what do you *have* to do, but what do you *get* to do?

Your vision of a perfect average day may look very different from the life you have today. For most people, it does. Then we go to step two, which is to take the next action, lay the next brick, keep breaking down your next actions into their smallest granular form. As coach Bill Walsh said, if you focus on these small, granular actions, the score takes care of itself. So take the smallest possible next action to keep moving forward towards your new desired reality—your pot of gold at the end of the rainbow.

Your perfect average day is your pot of gold at the end of the rainbow, where you have the time, energy, relationships, and money that you really want. Notice that you don't live your life by the year, month, or week. You live your life one day at a time.

For instance, you get up, you do things, you go to bed, and then you get to do it all over again the next day. However, there's no guarantee of that. I'm not saying that to be morbid; I'm saying it because for approximately 160,000 people, today will be their last day on Earth.

That's why discovering how to manage your sources of energy will give you the power to break through obstacles, conquer life's challenges and triumph over adversity so you can confidently step into YOUR best future!

Afformations on Energy

Let me conclude this chapter with my top ten Afformations for leveraging energy.

1. Why do I leverage my physical energy so well?
2. Why do I love eating healthy foods?
3. Why do I love exercising and moving my body?
4. Why do I enjoy taking breaks and using goal-free zones?
5. Why do I know my Why-To's and Why-Not-To's?
6. Why do I know that I can do what I set out to do?
7. Why am I so confident?
8. Why do I know my purpose here on earth?
9. Why am I so grateful for the gifts of my life?
10. Why do I have so much to be grateful for?

Noah's Note

Remember that you have four sources of energy: physical, mental, emotional and spiritual. Not only are they all very important, they're interrelated. This means that you must practice to become more proficient at renewing all four sources of energy every day.

Renewing your energy is like recharging the battery in your phone: if you neglect to charge your phone battery, it stops working. It's the same with us humans. If you don't focus on renewing your sources of energy every day, you'll feel depleted, tired, and stressed-out.

The great news is that you CAN become proficient at renewing your four energy sources by following the steps I gave you in this chapter. When you do, you'll find that your life will become a lot happier, much easier and far more fulfilling as well!

4

Focus Factor 3: Leverage Your Relationships

How to Attract the Right People to Accelerate Your Life and Business

Everything you're going to do in your life and your business is going to happen with and through other human beings. It took me a long time to realize this. When I started working in corporate America many years ago, I honestly thought that if I just did a good job and kept my mouth shut, I would be recognized and promoted. In fact, I didn't put any focus or energy into building relationships, because I truly believed that merit was the key to success.

Boy, was I wrong. I finally realized that it doesn't work that way at all in the real world. I'm sure you and I can point to example after example where the best person for the job didn't get promoted, while the person who plays the game best got the promotion. That's why, whether you have a job or you own your own business, you must become very good at leveraging relationships if you truly want to succeed.

Win Cubed Thinking

To begin with, every human being does what they feel is in their own best interest at every minute.

Consequently, you cannot get someone to do something that they don't want to do in the first place. You can't manipulate people. Even if you're getting them to do something that they didn't want to do, they actually *did* want to do it at some level.

Stephen Covey talked about thinking win-win. He was totally right, but I like to talk about win-win-win: I win, you win, and the world wins. There's a larger win, which goes back to the topic of purpose. The triple win gets people very excited: We're not just making money. We're not just making a difference. We're changing the world.

That's another reason Steve Jobs got people excited: he said, "We're not just selling computers. We're not selling phones. We're changing the world." He was a master at the triple win. He probably realized, "Let's see. I could sell computers and phones, or I could talk about changing the world." Which one do you think got people more excited?

To go back to personal relationships, if you have lots of money and no one to enjoy it with, you're like the widower I met at the Grand Canyon. When you are going through any experience, the thing that makes it valuable, memorable, and happy is the fact that you're sharing it with someone else. Imagine having a great win and celebrating all by yourself. You'll ask, "What is the point of this?"

It is a natural thing to think that everybody's just in it for themselves. To a degree, that is true. Nearly a century ago, Dale Carnegie wrote that everything that we humans do is based on something that we want. We want it, so we do it.

THIS IS HOW TO GET PEOPLE EXCITED TO JOIN YOUR CAUSE.

He was totally right, but that in and of itself is a very limited way of thinking.

To going back to the win-win that I was talking about, it's not wrong; it's not bad. But what if we even had a larger win? Wouldn't that be exciting, especially today, when we desperately need change and transformation? We need to raise the consciousness of the earth. That's why I talk about raising the consciousness of humanity, one question at a time. Do you think humanity might need a consciousness reset right now? I would say we do.

The number one thing in relationships is what Dale Carnegie said many years ago: think about what is important to the other person. Because guess what? That person does not care about me. Maybe they like me. Maybe they are entertained by me, but do they really care about what I want? Not really, unless it involves what they want.

THIS IS WHY IT'S CRUCIAL TO THINK ABOUT WHAT THE OTHER PERSON WANTS.

There's nothing wrong with that. Some complain that people are selfish. That's true, but that doesn't mean we're bad. Selfish and bad are not the same thing at all, although of course selfishness taken to an extreme is not a great idea.

For example, whenever I'm coaching an individual, group or team, whether in person or virtually, I focus on helping them get what's important to them. My thought is, *How can I help them get what they want while also getting what I want?*

You know how it feels when you're talking with someone who drones on and on about themselves vs. talking with someone who seems genuinely interested in you? That feeling goes both ways. Be the person who's interested in others and you'll quickly rise to the top of your industry. As Zig Ziglar said: help more people get what they want, and you'll get more of what you want.

The Right People

In relationships, it's a matter of attracting the right people and putting off the wrong people. When I say the right people, I mean people who are helping you get what you want while you are helping them get what they want.

The wrong people drain our energy and do not build our self-confidence. Sometimes it's a matter of people who are very close to you: family, extended family. This has been one of the biggest mistakes that I've made in my life: spending too much time with and pouring tons of energy into what I call *energy vampires*. An energy vampire is someone who sucks the energy, the life out of you. I spent way too much time on them because I thought I could fix them. I thought I could help them, and I was wrong every single time.

Let me give you an example with extended family. We were having a party at our house, which I've just moved into recently. It's beautiful, and I'm thrilled that I have the opportunity to live there. My clients call it Success Manor. I'm very protective of Success Manor and am very careful about the energy and the people that I allow in.

At this party, there was one particular family member that was rubbing everyone the wrong way. He's a very abrasive person, and everybody knows it. He bothered everyone, not just me.

I let it go one time. The second time it happened, I said to my wife, "I am revoking his Success Manor privileges," meaning he's not allowed in my house anymore. My wife totally agreed. That was not hard for me, and I was very happy about that. Previously, I would have said nothing; I would have let him run roughshod over me. I was proud that I stood up for myself and what I want: "This is my house. And no, you can't act like that in my house."

I'll give you another example. I was working with a client who was very difficult. Everything was a complaint; nothing was ever good enough. I was giving him the same training I give everyone else: everyone else was thrilled; everyone else was happy. At first, I went overboard, trying to please him.

Every day, I would wake up, and I would dread getting an email from this person. Finally, he sent an email that was abusive not only to me, but to my team.

THIS IS HOW TO REPEL ENERGY VAMPIRES.

That was the last straw. I thought, "Why are you doing this? Just give him his money back and get rid of him." So I fired him and gave him his money back, because I realized that I was allowing him to be an energy vampire in my life. As a result of that one action (firing the client), I felt free! I was so happy because I felt that I'd gotten an 800-pound gorilla off my chest.

Since that experience, I've never had a client treat me or my team like that again. And if a negative person somehow manages get through our meticulous application process (which is now much more rigorous, in order to weed out problem clients), today we have a process to fire them in days, instead of weeks.

Bottom line: Get rid of the energy vampires in your life, and realize you have much more power than you think.

Five Energy Support Systems

Let me go on to my 7-figure relationship secrets.

Secret number one: *install your systems of support*. In order for us to achieve our goals, certain systems have to be in place and functioning properly, just as blood has to flow through your body in order for you to live. Similarly, your business, relationships, or wealth can't grow or even survive if you don't have these systems in place. These are the five essential systems of support:

1. People
2. Activities
3. Environment
4. Introspection
5. Simplification

If we don't have these systems properly in place, we're going to have bottlenecks. A bottleneck is a point in your business or your life where energy, information, customers, and/or money are not flowing properly. It is crucial to understand these systems of support and to take the proper steps every day to install them.

Everything Happens through People

People are the most important part of the system. Everything flows through them. Having the wrong people on the bus is going to cause a bottleneck; so is having the right people in the wrong seats.

Earlier I mentioned my problems with email. So much of my day was being sucked up by email that I wasn't getting anything done. That was a symptom, but its cause was that I didn't have the right people in place.

If you're spending too much time on email, you're probably not able to focus on the three profit pillars I talked about earlier: getting more customers, increasing average order value, and increasing buyer frequency. That means you're being reactive instead of proactive, which means you don't have the right systems in place—and that means a lot of time, money, and opportunity are going to slip through your fingers.

I decided to hire a person to go through my emails. I told her, "Read my emails, and here are the responses that I want you to give." After all, 90 percent of the emails that we get are pretty much the same. Nine times out of ten, people are asking

THIS IS HOW TO STOP REINVENTING THE WHEEL.

one of ten or twenty questions. That's why they're called FAQs—frequently asked questions. You have a list of answers. You don't keep reinventing the wheel. You just send answer two or answer seven as needed. Everybody's happy, and you get more done in less time.

That's one simple example of how to install the people system. If you're wondering how to apply this to your business, ask, what things are you doing that you shouldn't be doing? How fast can you get the right people on the bus doing the right things in the right way for the right reasons?

Expand Your Sphere of Influence

Secret number two is *expand your sphere of influence*. Your sphere of influence is the number of people who know, like, and trust you. There's an old saying in business: it's not what you know; it's who you know. That's wrong. It's not who you know; it's who knows, likes, and trusts you. Even if I know the President of The United States, he may not know me yet. So it's not who you know, it's who knows you and who likes you and trusts you.

Back when I was working as a professional ballet dancer, my sphere of influence was that universe. When I had to retire because of a career-ending injury, I worked as a secretary, a janitor, and a waiter. I worked at a lot of jobs that weren't fulfilling, so my sphere of influence was very small. I started to work on expanding my sphere of influence, because I wanted more impact, influence, and income.

Your sphere of influence includes your friends, family, colleagues, team members, acquaintances, even authors of books that you like, or providers of seminars that you've attended. You may be thinking, "But I don't know anybody." OK; so you're a hermit living up in the mountains. Wrong! You probably know more people than you think. Your sphere of influence is probably larger than you think right now.

THIS IS HOW TO EXPAND YOUR SPHERE OF INFLUENCE.

The first step in expanding your sphere of influence is to write down what it is right now. Again, we're leveraging what we have to get more of what we want.

When you have your list, break it down into three types based on how much influence each person has:

1. **High influencers.** People who have a lot of influence. This can be through their email list, social media reach, podcast, and so on.
2. **Medium influencers.** They have a smaller but still pretty good audience.
3. **Those with low influence.** Regular people who don't necessarily have an audience per se.

Now go back and rate them by the amount they like you. Again, three categories:

1. They like you a lot.
2. They like somewhat: they could take or leave you.
3. They don't even know you.

That is the way to address and codify your current sphere of influence.

A quick story: in the early nineties, I was browsing in a church bookstore. All of a sudden, I heard something fall off a shelf. I looked down and picked up an audiocassette set. It was *The Seven Habits of Highly Effective People* by Stephen Covey. I looked around and wondered, how did that just fall off the shelf? Did the wind come in? I don't know how that happened, but I had never heard of that program before.

I listened to that series over and over. Tears were running down my face because I realized that I had been doing the seven habits of highly ineffective people for my whole life.

Years later, I got the opportunity to interview Dr. Covey, who gave me twenty uninterrupted minutes with him on the phone. It's something I'll never forget. I asked him, "Dr. Covey, how do you handle it when people worship you? When people say, you're the greatest thing in the world, how do you handle that?"

WHEN STEPHEN COVEY TOLD ME THIS SECRET, IT CHANGED MY LIFE.

He said something I'll never forget: "Noah, I want people to leave my seminars more impressed with themselves than with me." How rare is that? That's something that I strive to live by every day. It isn't about me, about how great Noah St. John is. It's about how we all have more power than we think.

Dr. Covey had a concept about influence that featured a small circle inside a larger circle. The small circle was labeled the *circle of influence*, and the larger circle was labeled the *circle of concern*. He said that most people put their focus on the wrong circle—concern—and end up shrinking their circle of influence.

Dr. Covey's point was very simple: most people are worried about things they can't control. When you do that, what are you doing? You are disempowering yourself simply by virtue of thinking the wrong thoughts: Why doesn't he do this? Why can't they do that? Why isn't that happening? Why am I getting this? Why isn't this happening? OK, that's something you are concerned about. But what are you going to do right now?

That's one reason why I'm so maniacally focused on what we *can* control—our thoughts, words, and actions. Every day, we can control them, whether you believe it or not. That was Dr. Covey's entire point about being proactive. Being proactive means we have the power, but we have to remember that fact. We often forget that I am in charge here. If I created this lousy situation, that means I can create the situation that I want.

Bring Value to Others

Secret number three is to *focus on bringing value to others*. List everything that you bring to the table that could be of value to the people in your sphere of influence. As I said, every human being at every moment is doing what they feel is in their own best interest at the time. In other words, no one is going to even talk to you if you don't bring value to them in some way.

An entrepreneur's most important goals are more profit and more freedom. We want more time, more energy, better relationships, and more money. So how can you help other people get more of those things? You can give advice. You can give tips, secrets, strategies, methods, contacts, and connections. List all the knowledge, secrets, and methods that you bring to the table that could be perceived as valuable to others. Then list the ways you can deliver that value.

BE VERY CLEAR ABOUT THE VALUE YOU BRING TO OTHERS.

You've got to be very specific about the value that you can bring to others. People are busy; they don't have time to understand what you do, and they can't read your mind. You've got to spell your value out for them in simple and clear language.

It's very important to be succinct. Have you ever been at networking events? You'll ask someone, what do you do? And they give you a twenty-seven-minute speech. Please, for the love of God, get that shorter, will you? People have short attention spans; get to the point, and don't give them your whole history. Remember that people love to buy, but they hate to be sold. So when you bring value to the table, you have to show them why it's in their best interest to give you money.

For example, my specialty is helping entrepreneurs, athletes, CEOs, thought leaders, consultants, coaches, authors, and speakers to make a lot more money in a lot less time with a lot less effort. I specialize in helping these groups because one of their biggest goals is to make more money in less time.

Since that's true, do you think a middle manager type of person will value what I do? Probably not, because they might not see how what I do will help them achieve their goals. That's why I'd rather stay within my specialty, because I know I can hit the ball out of the park every time and help my clients get remarkable results!

Focus on Perceived Value

Secret number four is to *focus on perceived value.* Did you realize that there is no such thing as absolute value? In fact, the only thing that's real is perceived value.

Let me give you an example. Imagine you have a juicy, sizzling, mouth-watering steak that you want to sell. Then you go and present it to a vegan. How's that sales presentation going to go? Clearly, you've got something that some people will value, while others (e.g., vegans) won't value it at all.

That's why you don't want to waste time "showing your steak to vegans." In this example, you want to show you steak to an omnivore—somebody who's going to appreciate what you bring to the table.

In the same vein, if you've got a great vegan dish and you're presenting it to an omnivore (someone who eats meat as well as vegetables), that's probably not going to so well, either.

Why all this talk about food? Because it makes the value example very clear. Now, who's right—vegans or omnivores? The obvious answer is that neither one is right or wrong. The simple truth is that different people value different things. The problem comes when you're trying to convince certain people to value something that they don't already value.

To go back to the truth of actual value vs. perceived value, many people would argue that teachers have the most important job in our society, yet they're not paid accordingly. On the other hand, professional sports figures are paid millions of dollars. While this doesn't make any sense from an actual value standpoint, it makes perfect sense from a perceived value standpoint, because sports professionals sell tickets, and those tickets sell food, tee shirts, and merchandise—which is why professional sports is a multibillion-dollar industry.

Is it fair that teachers are paid so much less than professional sports figures? No, but that disparity highlights the truth of actual value vs. perceived value in the marketplace.

Here's another example. Let's say you have knowledge and experience that you've accumulated over your lifetime—knowledge that can help others. What should you do? Well, you can package your knowledge in the form of books, online courses, virtual events or seminars, so that other people can benefit from your knowledge and experience.

For example, what do entrepreneurs value? Profit and freedom.

What do CEOs value? In most cases, shareholder value.

What do professional athletes value? Having an edge over their competition.

What do spouses value? Love and attention.

What do children value? Love, time, and attention.

These are examples of what different types of people value and therefore, what you could conceivably package and sell to different groups of people. Therefore, the better you get at understanding perceived value and creating packages to bring that value to others, the more money you can make and the greater impact you can have in the world!

Get Referrals

Secret number five is to *get referrals*. Think about what a referral is. A referral is someone offering a resource to someone they know, like, and trust, and who knows, likes, and trust them. When you see a great movie, what do you do? You tell your friends about it. You've just made a referral. Why did that work? Because your friend trusts your judgment. They believe that you are not going to steer them wrong. We've done it with restaurants, TV shows, cars, sneakers, clothes. That's why it is crucial to get referrals so that we are instantly positioned as having high value.

Think about the two ways to grow a business. You can pay for advertising; nothing wrong with that. But imagine the power of referrals from people who already know, like, and trust you.

The power is tenfold or even more. When somebody clicks on an ad and goes to your website, are they going to trust you? Probably not; almost certainly not. They're probably skeptical; they've probably been burned many times.

THIS IS WHY REFERRALS BEAT PAID ADVERTISING.

With referrals, someone says, "You really need to check

out this person. He's great." "Really? What's his website? Let me check him out."

You see what's happened? Because I know I can trust that friend, you've been instantly positioned as having high value. That goes back to my earlier point that there is no absolute value; there's only perceived value. Because you want to be positioned as high value, getting referrals is crucial. It's the cheapest way to grow your business, because essentially it costs nothing.

As I've already emphasized, it's important is to ask for what you want. In order to increase your referrals, you just have to ask for them. Of course, this assumes you're doing good work. That's a big assumption, because many people, as we know, aren't.

To increase your referral ability, you have to provide actual value to human beings. But that's not enough. You also have to ask for them, because people are busy. They're not going to just assume, "I think I should give Noah a referral today." Why would they think that? That's what's important to me, not what's important to them. How do you make it important to them? You ask.

You also tell them about your larger mission. I myself have a purpose: to create 1,000 new millionaires in the next three years. Can you help me with that? Do you know someone who would like to live The 7-Figure Life? If you like my work, please send them my way, and I will take great care of them. That's another important point that you need to make: I will take great care of whoever you send to me.

People don't necessarily think, "Noah is so great. He's really doing a great job." When a customer has a complaint, they're ten times more likely to complain than someone who's happy, who is more likely to say nothing. The happy people probably won't say anything, and the unhappy people will tell everybody. Again, it's not fair, it's not right, but that's human nature. So we have to, in a sense, fight human nature by saying, "If you have gotten value from this relationship, can you think of anyone else who will benefit from the work that we've done together?" Ninety-nine times out of 100, people will say yes.

You can also have affiliate marketing: when it's appropriate, you can also pay affiliate commissions. When people refer someone to you, you can pay them a commission

THIS IS HOW TO JOIN OUR AFFILIATE PROGRAM FOR FREE.

based on the referral's purchase of a product or service. Our company has an affiliate program in place. Because that is a client I wouldn't have gotten on my own,

I'm happy to pay the affiliate fee. You can sign up for my affiliate program for free at **www.NoahStJohn.com/jv.**

Deliver On the Small Things

Secret number six is *deliver on the small things.* Delivering on the small things means doing things like showing up on time, finishing what you start, and delivering what you say you're going to deliver.

Let me ask you a question. In your experience, how many people have actually done what they said they would do? The sad truth is that millions of people people have been ripped off by the gurus just like I was. That's the bad news.

However, the good news is that because so many people have been ripped off by gurus, liars and scam artists, as long as you do what say you're going to do both in your personal and professional life, you will instantly rise above your competition—simply because it's so rare these days!

Of course, there are always going to be problems and mishaps. I sell a lot of online programs, and I've had people who simply did not get the email that had the program we sent. Sometimes that email gets lost. Of course we sent it, but it's gotten lost in a spam trap or whatever it might be. The customer is indignant: "You're a rip-off artist. I'm going to tell everybody."

In those cases, I will call the customer (yes, actually pick up the phone!) and say, "I understand you didn't get the email we sent you. Let me help you with that."

I'm *communicating in words* that my company did what we said we would (fulfilled our promise), and *demonstrating through actions* that we actually CARE about our clients and customers.

That's why I'll say, "I understand you didn't get the email we sent you, and I want to make sure you're taken care of right away. Do you have another email address I can send your program to?"

What have I just done? First, I've acknowledged that they have a problem. I've acknowledged their complaint, their concern. Naturally, when somebody buys something, they want to get what they paid for, so they have every right to be upset if they don't receive it. That's why the customer lashed out, because there are so many rip-off artists out there and perhaps they've been burned in the past.

However, when I call my customers, I gain *superfans*—because that simple act demonstrates that I actually care. Prior to that, the customer was justifiably upset because they hadn't received access to the program they bought. Now, they get the experience of talking to someone (a thought leader) who actually cares about them.

However, as a result of me taking the time to call them (something that most thought leaders simply don't do), the client now understands that I did in fact deliver on my promise and that it was a simple case of a missing email.

THIS IS HOW TO GAIN SUPERFANS.

As a result of that small but significant action, they get to *experience* the level of commitment I have to my clients and their well-being, as well as my dedication to deliver on my promises.

That's a simple but powerful example of how you can listen to people and take care of them. Just having that human touch goes far. As the saying goes: "There are no traffic jams along the extra mile."

With referrals, you just keep adding value and keep asking, and eventually they'll come around. Of course a VIP is busy and has lots of other things to do. They may not know you from Adam. You just have to keep providing value.

For example, you see an article in *Inc.* or *Entrepreneur* related to that influencer's field of expertise. Mail them the article with a hand-written note: "I saw this article and thought you might enjoy it." Even if they're not in the article, when it's about something they might appreciate, this approach can work wonders because so few people do it.

You don't even ask for anything. That raises your perceived value. Everybody goes to VIPs with their hands out. If you don't act that way and instead are the person giving, you will stand out in a great way.

You can also forward a connection to someone else. Important people like to meet other important people. If you link this person up with someone who might be a great connection for them, you're raising your perceived value even more.

Afformations on Relationships

Here are my top ten Afformations for leveraging relationships.

1. Why is it OK for me to get what I want?
2. Why do I love making other people feel important?
3. Why do I love giving value to others?
4. Why do other people see the value that I bring?
5. Why do I love having the right people in my life?
6. Why am I such a blessing to others?
7. Why do the right people come into my life now?
8. Why do I easily attract the right people to help me reach my goals?
9. Why am I so grateful for the people in my life?

10. Why do I have so many amazing, supportive, wonderful friends?

Noah's Note

You CAN become proficient at leveraging your relationships, both in your personal life as well as your professional life. If a shy nerd like me can do it, you can do it, too.

Yes, it takes time and practice to master the secrets in this chapter. It won't happen overnight. However, when you realize the enormous difference this will make in your life, your business, and your legacy, that will give you the right Why-To to keep persisting, even in the face of challenges or adversity.

Use the secrets in this chapter to leverage your relationships, and watch your life, career and business skyrocket as a result!

5

Focus Factor 4: Leveraging Your Money

How to Use What You Have to Get More of What You Want

When most people think about living The 7-Figure Life, money is the first thing that comes to mind. However, in my coaching as well as my online courses, I focus on helping people leverage time, energy, and relationships *before* money; not because money is the least important element, but to show people why it's important to focus on all Four Focus Factors that I discuss.

For example:

- *Time* is the most valuable resource because it's the only one that's finite (money can always be replaced).

- *Energy* is critical because without it, you're either not alive or you're simply not happy (no matter how much money you have).

- *Relationships* are crucial because all money comes from other people (you have some money and everyone else has all the rest).

As I stated earlier in this book, if I gave you a million dollars tomorrow and told you that the conditions were that you couldn't have any time to enjoy it; you had to be *unhappy* all the time; and that you couldn't enjoy it with anyone—I think most people would agree that that doesn't sound like a great deal at all. That's why I help my clients to leverage all Four Focus Factors in order to truly live The 7-Figure Life.

Also, when you look at the Four Focus Factors of time, energy, relationships, and money, they spell the acronym TERM. If I put money first, it would be MTRE, which doesn't work very well. This means that, even if you didn't do well in school, this is a TERM paper that we all really would love to get an A on!

Earlier, I told you that I grew up poor in a rich neighborhood and as a result of following my own system, have now created a lifestyle of health, wealth and happiness for myself and my family. Mae West said, "I've been rich, and I've been poor, and rich is better." I completely agree with that sentiment. Because I lived through it, I can tell you unequivocally that there's nothing inherently good about poverty.

For example, many people think it's more spiritual to be poor than to be rich. However, it's simply not true. Money merely acts as a magnifying glass. As I've already pointed out, poor jerks who get money become rich jerks—only jerkier. Spiritual, loving, generous people who are poor at one time become more generous, loving, and more giving if they get money later.

Here's another example: in the movies, the bad guy is often depicted as a wealthy, greedy businessman. While of course we can find plenty of examples of wealthy businesspeople who are greedy, you can also find plenty of examples of wealthy businesspeople who are generous, charitable and who support worthy causes.

THIS IS A MAJOR CAUSE OF HEAD TRASH ABOUT MONEY.

For instance, when I was poor, all of my friends were poor, because that's where my consciousness was. Today, all of my friends are wealthy AND they're really cool people. It's easy to find greedy jerks who have a lot of money, but you can also find greedy jerks who don't have any money. The irony is that whether someone has a lot of money has little to do with whether someone is a good person or not. The money is simply going to magnify what was already there in the first place.

The Money Mindset

Most of what I'm teaching about money has to do with the mindset around it—the beliefs, as well as the head trash, around money. Many people have a lot of head trash saying, "I can't be happy and rich," or, "I can't be a rich person and a good person." For most people, this is what's causing them to stop themselves. For example, I helped a client who was stuck to increase his income over 600% in under a year. That "hockey stick growth" didn't happen because I taught him about investments or bitcoin. That remarkable growth happened because I helped him take out his head trash.

Good Debt, Bad Debt

Some advisers preach a debt-free, low-to-no-leverage approach to building wealth: pay off your mortgage as fast as you can, and be debt-free in your business from day one.

In fact, there is a big difference between good debt and bad debt. What's the difference? Debt is considered "bad" when it is unsecured debt, usually in the form of credit cards. For example, millions of Americans are carrying a large amount of credit card debt that they're trying to pay off every month. And since credit card companies charge high interest rates, this means that many people are never able to pay off their credit card debt. That's one reason why "Getting out of debt" is one of the most common money goals that people have.

Here's what I do to turn credit card debt from bad debt to good debt: I put most of my business expenses on a company credit card, and I pay it off in full every month. That way I never pay interest on my credit cards. In addition, I also receive points from the credit card companies based on my purchases for the month—and I use those points as either cash back or to purchase airline tickets.

Of course, when I started my business in 1997, I wasn't able to pay off my credit card bills in full every month because there wasn't enough money coming in to cover them. That's yet another reason to leverage the Four Focus Factors that I teach, so you can pay off your debt as soon as possible.

Another type of bad debt is student loan debt, which is very painful for millions of Americans. Even if you declare bankruptcy, you still have to pay it off. In 2022, President Biden forgave some of that debt, but of course future developments remain to be seen.

In The 7-Figure Lifestyle formula, play good offense and play good defense, just like in sports. A good offense means you're making money. A good defense is not overspending; you're not getting into bad, unsecured debt. You have to have a good offense and a good defense in order to win the game. Defense is more important than offense.

THIS IS WHY YOU NEED TO PLAY GOOD MONEY OFFENSE AND DEFENSE.

There's an old saying in football: "Defense wins championships." If you are making $1 million a year and spending $2 million, that's not great. Although you've got to have offense—you've got to make money—you also have to live below your means.

Banks are not going to be any help at all. In most cases, if as an entrepreneur you go into a bank and ask for a loan, they're going to ask you for so much collateral. The classic joke about a banker is that they're someone who gives you their umbrella when it's sunny and wants it back when it's raining.

For most entrepreneurs, it's a waste of time to go to a traditional bank for a business loan. Nowadays there are so many more lending choices out there online that you don't even need to have a business plan or any of the things that were necessary in the olden days. It is easier to get money now today than ever before. However, the challenge is that you must play good offense (making enough profit), play good defense (spend less than you bring in), and avoid the high interest fees that will keep you in debt for longer than necessary.

Get In the Right Quadrant

Let's get into my ten money leveraging secrets. Secret number one to leverage your money is to *get in the right quadrant of the Income-Happiness Matrix*. Here's what I mean by that: all of us want more money, and everyone wants to be happier. That's because money without happiness is meaningless, yet it's awfully hard to be happy when you don't have enough money.

However, here is the problem: most people are chasing money and they're chasing happiness, yet the more you chase these things, the more they tend to go away. Rather than chasing money or happiness, we have to chase the things that cause them and put them into place in our daily lives.

What then causes income and happiness? There are two factors involved: *activities* and *aptitude*. *Activities* means, what are you doing with the hours of your day? *Aptitude* means, how good are you at doing them, and how much do you enjoy them?

The Income-Happiness Matrix

Golden handcuffs Low aptitude, high value	Freedom Lifestyle High aptitude, high value
Busywork Low aptitude, low value	Hobby High aptitude, low value

I created The Income-Happiness Matrix based on these four elements. We have two types of activities: low-value and high-value. There are two types of aptitude: things you're lousy at and things that you're great at. In the lower right quadrant, we have low-value activities that you're great at and enjoy. That's the *hobby quadrant*.

Here's the problem: many people think they have a business when they really have a hobby. There's nothing wrong with having hobbies. We should all have hobbies: life is not about working all the time. However, the question I often ask business owners is: *Do you own a business, or do you own a hobby?*

The second quadrant is the lower left, where you have low-value activities that you're lousy at and don't enjoy. That is the area of lowest value, both in activities and aptitude. That's the *busywork quadrant*.

In business, especially when you're just starting out, there are times when you have to do certain activities that could qualify as busywork. For example, checking email, doing social media, bookkeeping, and managing client files could be classified as busywork, because you might not enjoy these very much and they might not directly add to your bottom line.

Yes, there are certain tasks that must be completed in order to keep the lights on in your business. However, that doesn't mean that you should be the one doing them. Just like when I talked about outsourcing in an earlier chapter, it's vital that you hire someone who will do these kinds of tasks as soon as possible, if you want to scale up to the next level in your enterprise.

Then you have the high-value activities that you're bad at and don't really enjoy. That's the *golden handcuffs quadrant.*

I'll give you an example. A married couple hired me to coach them. She had her own business, and he was working at a job. He was making good money. He was making six figures a year, but he hated it, so he was very unhappy. He was sick all the time. He was working in a manufacturing firm, and his back hurt. He was always in pain, but he said, "I can't quit, because I've got to take care of my family" (they had four kids). They were in the golden handcuffs quadrant, and he felt trapped.

As a result of coaching with me and following my system, the husband was finally able to quit his job and transition from the golden handcuffs quadrant to the fourth quadrant, which is the one we want to spend most of our time in. That is the area of high-value activities that you're great at and that you love. That's *the Freedom Lifestyle Quadrant.*

When you're in the Freedom Lifestyle Quadrant, you're serving the world, adding value to your clients and customers, and enjoying more income, more impact, and more influence. In fact, when you follow my system, one of the best results is that you'll get to spend the majority of your waking hours in the Freedom Lifestyle Quadrant—which is like going to heaven without the inconvenience of dying!

That's why one of the most important goals for an entrepreneur is to spend 75 percent of your time in the Freedom Lifestyle Quadrant. There's no way around the fact that if you are not doing high-value activities that you great at and that you love, you're simply not going to be living that Freedom Lifestyle.

Therefore, now let's go through some exercises to help you spend more of your day, more of your time, and more of your life in the Freedom Lifestyle Quadrant, so you too can get to heaven without the inconvenience of dying.

Determine How You Spend Your Time

Secret number two to leverage your money is to *determine how you spend our time.* If you own your own business, then you are going to find yourself in one of these four lifestyle quadrants. In other words, you're either going to be in the hobby quadrant (high aptitude/low value), busywork quadrant (low aptitude/ low value), golden handcuffs quadrant (low aptitude/ high value), or Freedom Lifestyle Quadrant (high aptitude/high value). That's it. There's really nowhere else to go.

Write down how much time you spend in each quadrant per week. Do this on a percentage basis. On a percentage basis, how much time of your work week do you spend in each quadrant?

Let's start with the *hobby quadrant*. What percentage of your week are you currently spending in the hobby quadrant? For example, when I am working in my garden with my wife, I am not directly focusing on making money or building my business during that time. Working in my garden is something I enjoy (high aptitude/enjoyment) that doesn't have any perceived value to anyone but me and my wife. That's why no one is going to pay me money for working in my own garden!

However, what if you're spending your time working, yet you're not making any money? In that case, you probably own a hobby and not a business. I want you to be very clear on this point.

Therefore, write the percentage of your workweek that you're currently spending in the hobby quadrant (from zero percent to 100 percent).

Next, I want you to write what percentage of your week is spent in the *busywork quadrant*. Remember that's the lowest-value quadrant, the

THIS IS HOW TO ESCAPE THE LOW VALUE QUADRANTS.

one that you need to get yourself out of as quickly as possible. The fact is that many entrepreneurs tell me that they're spending up to 75 percent of their workweek in the busywork quadrant. The problem with that is, it's like going to hell without the inconvenience of dying.

Then we have the golden handcuffs quadrant. That's what I was talking about with the client I mentioned above. He realized that he was spending his whole life in golden handcuffs and could never escape unless he did something different. We helped him start a landscaping business. He was scared to leave his job, but he was able to do it. He transitioned successfully from the job he hated, and now he's making more money than before. He gets to spend his time outdoors and with his family, and he is happier than ever. That is what can happen when you transition to a freedom lifestyle.

Finally, write the percentage of your workweek that you get to spend in the *Freedom Lifestyle Quadrant*. That's where you're doing high value activities that you love, that you're great at, and that people pay you money for. You'll know when you're in this awesome quadrant because you can become so immersed in a task or project that you lose track of time.

Have you ever been so caught up in doing something (like, for example, writing a book) that hours go by and you don't even notice? That's when you know that you're in the Freedom Lifestyle Quadrant.

THIS IS HOW TO LIVE A FREEDOM LIFESTYLE.

Whatever It Takes

Secret number three to leverage your money is to *do whatever it takes*. Now that you have your percentages of how much time you spend each week in each lifestyle quadrant, now I want you to list ten reasons why you are going to do *whatever it takes* to spend a minimum of 75 percent of your workweek in the Freedom Lifestyle Quadrant.

When I do this exercise with my clients, nobody has ever said that they're spending 75 percent of their time in the Freedom Lifestyle Quadrant. They'll say, "Wow, I didn't realize that I'm spending almost no time in the Freedom Lifestyle Quadrant, and I'm spending most of my time in the busywork, handcuffs or hobby quadrants."

The numbers don't lie. They will tell whether you are doing activities that are creating the income that you desire. So this is a stunningly simple and effective way to look at where you're spending the hours of your work week and move to the Freedom Lifestyle Quadrant.

Some have asked whether you can release yourself from those handcuffs and remain an employee. Absolutely—as long as you love your job. If you love your job, great. My role is not to say you shouldn't have a job and you're a dummy if you don't start your own business. Many gurus do that; they say you're an idiot if you don't start your own business. But who are they to say that? Who are they to tell people what to do and what not to do? My job is to provide options.

If you love your job and are making good money, why leave it? However, if you hate your job, even if you're making good money, you've got a choice to make. Are you going to stick with the job you hate?

This takes us back to the factor of energy: "I'm sad. I'm angry. I'm resentful every day." That's a lousy way to go through life. So that is the factor. Do you enjoy your job? If you do, more power to you; keep doing it and keep adding more value to more people.

AFOS or HSBO?

Secret number four to leverage your money is to *stop acting like an AFOS and start acting like a HSBO.* AFOS stands for *average frustrated opportunity seeker,* and HSBO (pronounced HIS-bo) stands for *highly successful business owner.*

How do you know if you're acting like an AFOS? Here are some symptoms: Are you constantly chasing shiny objects, of which there are trillions out there? There are infinite choices, infinite distractions, and that's bad news for the AFOS.

Do you find it easy to start projects and hard or impossible to finish them? The problem with not finishing what you start is that you don't get paid at the start; you get paid at the finish. That's why, if you're acting like an AFOS, you might have twenty different projects going on, yet nothing is ever done. That's why the word frustrated is part of the description—because, if you're doing this, you're probably feeling very frustrated by your lack of results.

How do you know if you are a HSBO? First of all, HSBOs employ systems that run on autopilot. To go back to the analogy of the team owner, you want to be the one who has the players doing the work. It doesn't have to be humans: you can use automated systems running on autopilot.

If you are a HSBO, you stop sacrificing time for dollars. If you're sacrificing time for dollars, you have a ceiling on your income. Also, HSBOs receive most of the recognition and financial rewards. You get to enjoy transforming lives around the world. You get to have the impact, the influence, and the income that is reserved only for the HSBO.

Right now, list three to five ways that you've been acting like an AFOS. Do you have shiny object syndrome? Do you have dozens of unfinished projects? Do you find it hard to stay focused? Are you spending too much time working without enjoying life? Those are some symptoms of AFOS-ness.

Then write how that has affected you, your family, business, legacy, impact, influence, and income. This will show you the cost of acting like an AFOS.

At this point, the world is conspiring to create more AFOS. Social media platforms are designed to keep you on them. They have engineers, psychologists, and many other people working to make sure you don't leave. They show advertising; that's how they make their money. Their job is to keep you addicted. That's just one simple example.

TO BREAK YOUR ADDICTIONS, YOU NEED A STRONGER WHY-TO.

In order to break those addictions, we have to have a stronger Why-To. What is your priority? Why do you want to be a HSBO? Write down three to five reasons why you want to start acting like a HSBO right now and you're not going to be derailed by distractions.

People ask me, how did you write eighteen books? By writing them. But the deeper answer is, because

I decided to. Because I want my message out. Some would say that's arrogance. I would say no; it's just what I felt like doing. And I had to believe in myself before anyone believed in me. That was hard. Now that I have people who also believe in me, it's a lot easier. In fact, the numbers don't lie: before I had the right support system, I only published one book. Since I've had the support system in place, I've published over eighteen books in many languages. That's how you go from being an AFOS to being a HSBO.

The Power of Automation

Secret number five to leverage your money is to *automate systems that can run on autopilot*. For example, I sell a lot of digital online programs. I couldn't possibly do that without systems that run on autopilot. So what I love about the digital age is that you build it once and you sell it till the end of time.

AFOS don't do that. They take lots of courses. They have lots of shelf-help. They learn without earning. They keep thinking, "I just have to learn a little bit more." You probably know enough by now to put something together. You

THIS IS HOW YOU CAN BUILD SOMETHING ONCE AND SELL IT FOREVER.

might need a little help; certainly we all need help at certain times. But the point is that you've got to build something that you can then sell.

For example, I created an online course called *Power Habits® Academy*. I created it one time, and I've sold it thousands of times. Instead of putting in X number of hours and getting Y amount of dollars, I put in a small amount of work at the beginning, and now I can make as much as I want until the end of time. That's one simple example of what you should automate.

Naturally, there are certain responsibilities that can't be completely automated, like leadership, mentorship, sales and marketing. However, there are aspects of these tasks that you *can* automate. For example, over the last twenty-five years, I've created thousands of hours of content through my videos, virtual events and keynote speeches. Rather than spending my time posting on social media (something I consider to be busywork), I trained my team to post my content on my social media accounts.

Why? Because I simply don't enjoy posting on social media for hours a day. Now I understand that posting on social media does excite some people. If that's you, then by all means do it. However, I'd rather be leveraging my time by mentoring individuals and teams to even greater success.

People often ask how long it should take for you to see some substantial financial rewards as you make that transition. The numbers don't lie. Before I had this process in place—the first ten years of my business—I never broke six figures, because I didn't have these things in place. As soon as I got them in place, I broke six figures the first year, and it's been going up and up since then. This year, we are up ten times from the previous year.

THIS IS HOW WE HELP PEOPLE MAKE SEVEN AND EIGHT FIGURES IN RECORD TIME.

One client, Steven, came to me and wanted to transition. He was not necessarily in golden handcuffs, because he enjoyed what he did, but he wanted to start his own business. He wanted more impact, more influence, more income. I helped him put this system in place. His income increased 800 percent in just twelve weeks. It can really happen.

The Four Wealth Vehicles

Secret number six to leverage your money is to *understand the four wealth vehicles*. I look at wealth as a destination. When you want to reach a destination, you normally take a vehicle: a bicycle, a car, a van, a plane. There are four basic vehicles that you can use to attain wealth:

1. **Your retirement account.** An IRA, a 401(k), and similar vehicles.

2. **Real estate.** You'll learn about the two types of real estate in secret number eight.

3. **Investments.** Cryptocurrency, Bitcoin, stocks, bonds, art, jewelry—your typical investment vehicles.

4. **Your own business.** Owning your own business is the most common way for people to reach the destination called wealth.

Now that you know the four wealth vehicles, I want you to list the vehicles you're currently using to get wealthy and how much money you currently have in each.

For instance, how much is in your retirement account? Are you investing in real estate? Do you have other investments? Do you own your own business? Or, do you have a combination of two or more of the wealth vehicles?

The fact is, you can use any combination of these four wealth vehicles to get wealthy—it's really up to you.

However, if you don't take out your head trash about money, it's like you're driving along the road of life with one foot on the brake. For instance, imagine that you're driving to your destination, but you unconsciously have one foot on the brake. You begin to notice that you're not going as fast as you want, so you start searching for advice.

Guru number one comes along and says to you, "The problem is that you're using the wrong gas. Try this expensive high-octane gas." You go to the gas station and spend money to fill up your tank with expensive high-octane. However, because you still have one foot on the brake, you're still not reaching your destination very quickly.

The second guru comes along saying, "These tires aren't good enough. Get a new set of tires." You get expensive tires and put them on your car. You're spending more money. You get back in the car, but you still have your foot on the brake, so you're still getting the same result.

The third guru comes along, saying, "You need to get a new car. You should get an expensive sports car like mine. These are the best cars in the world. They cost a lot of money, but you'll look great, you'll feel great, and you'll get to your destination faster."

You think, "Well, he's popular on social media, so he must know what he's talking about." So you spend a ton of money and trade in your perfectly

HERE'S WHAT I DO THAT'S DIFFERENT FROM THE GURUS.

good car for a expensive sports car. You get in your new car, but you're still doing the same thing, so you still get the same results.

Here's what I do that's different: I say, "Did you know you have your foot on the brake?"

"No," you say.

"Do you know that if you take your foot off the brake, you can reach your goals faster and with a lot less effort? That's why my clients are able to make more in twelve weeks than they made in the previous twelve months, while still gaining one to three hours a day and four to eight weeks per year."

"That sounds great!" you say. "Where do I sign up?" (See Recommended Resources at the back of this book, or visit **BreakthroughwithNoah.com.**)

That's what makes my system different, and it's why we've helped so many people add six, seven and eight figures while winning their lives back. If you're not reaching your goals as fast as you want, it's not about buying better gas, better tires, or even a new car.

What makes my system different (and what gives my clients an unfair advantage) is that we give you the right plan, the right tools and the right support so you can stop driving along the road of life with one foot on the brake.

In fact, my system removes the hidden cause of the problem, rather than just talking about symptoms, which is why my clients get such transformational, remarkable and life-changing results.

It's All Math

Secret number seven is *all wealth comes down to math*. For example, if you have credit card debt and you're not able to pay it off in full every month—meaning you have interest that is accruing—you must address that first. Whether you have a retirement account or even investments, you're not probably going to get 22 percent rate of increase consistently. But you are going to get hammered by 22 percent or more by the credit card companies. That's definite. You are pouring water in one end, and water is leaking out the other.

In this case, I would focus 80 percent on paying off the credit cards. Remember that good old 80-20 rule: 80 percent paying down the debt and 20 percent investing. You could just as easily use 100 percent to pay off your debt, and you wouldn't be wrong. But if you only use your money to pay down the debt, it doesn't feel as good as saving. When I see my money piling up, that's a good feeling. Paying down debt is also a good feeling, but it's not the same. It's less pain, but the investment piling up means more pleasure.

Another obvious point: if you work for a company and are getting a match for a 401(k) or something similar, at the very least you should be contributing up to what they're matching. That's free money.

I feel that everyone should have a retirement account, because we're living longer than ever before. None of us know when it's our last day, so we have to hope for the best and prepare for the worst. I don't want to work my whole life. I definitely want to retire. At what age? I have a certain age earmarked. There are plenty of free retirement calculators online, and you can just type in the numbers.

You definitely want to have a retirement account and be funding it every month, even if it's $50 a month or $20 a month. As is often said, compound interest is the most powerful force in the universe. Unfortunately, in some cases, returns on retirement accounts tend to be less than inflation. For most people, retirement savings won't be enough, especially as we are living longer. My job is to show you these four wealth vehicles so that you can make intelligent choices based on your own situation.

Building Your Real Estate Wealth

Secret number eight is *leverage your real estate holdings*. Over the last twenty-five years, I've helped my clients make hundreds of millions of dollars in real estate. Ironically, I don't teach "how to make money in real estate." Instead, I teach "how to stop stopping yourself from making money in real estate." In other words, I teach the Inner Game of real estate success, which is why my clients consistently add six, seven, and eight figures, no matter what the market is doing.

THIS IS HOW TO INCREASE THE VALUE OF YOUR VIRTUAL REAL ESTATE.

Today there are two forms of real estate: physical real estate, such as land and properties; and virtual real estate, meaning Internet domains and online properties that you own. For example, I own over 300 Internet domains that I've been building and scaling since 1997.

Of course, some of these domains are more valuable than others. That's because the classic real estate truth holds true online as well as offline: why does an acre in downtown Manhattan cost a lot more than an acre in Butte, Montana? Location, location, location.

It's the same with digital real estate. For instance, the most valuable digital real estate are domains like Amazon, Apple, Google, YouTube, and Facebook, which all started from nothing and are today worth untold billions of dollars.

Of course, most of us won't build properties with that kind of valuation. However, I do teach my clients that it's crucial to own your own virtual real estate and increase its value over time. That's the beauty of virtual real estate: you can buy something for a very small amount of money and increase its value over time, by adding value to the marketplace and to other human beings.

I started my company, SuccessClinic.com, in a 300-square-foot basement apartment with $800 and a book on HTML back in 1997. Now it's worth a lot of money, because I created a lot of value. It doesn't have to take that long. My clients are able to get there faster than I did because I've been doing it for so long, and I have the scars, scrapes, and bruises to show for it. In any case, you can have both physical and digital real estate, but you have to know what you're doing. And of course you have to focus so that you can get the results that you want.

Some people do real estate investing on a part-time basis for extra income. Generally, I believe that if you're in a business or career, you're better off pouring more attention into that than dividing yourself between a business and part-time real estate. Is it wrong to do real estate part-time? Of course not, if that's what you want, but

THIS IS WHY IT'S CRUCIAL TO UNDERSTAND YOUR OWN RISK TOLERANCE.

you've got to realize that sometimes you have to rob Peter to pay Paul. Is it worth the trade? That's something you'd have to decide for yourself.

Understand Your Risk Tolerance

Secret number nine to leverage your money is to *understand your risk tolerance*. Personally I am very risk-averse, probably because I grew up poor, and I'm afraid of losing money. See, that's one of my fears. That fear has cost me money over time by keeping me from investing in different vehicles.

For example, I don't have a lot invested in the stock market at the moment because the market is very volatile right now. Many years ago when I was in the market in a heavy way, it was also very volatile. I was anxious all the time. I couldn't sleep. My stomach was upset. Finally I just called my wealth advisor and said, "Just get me out of the market." I cashed out because I couldn't take it. Did I lose money? Probably, but I felt better.

At least now I understood my risk tolerance, which is very low. Others will have a high risk tolerance. So make sure you understand and know your own risk tolerance. What are you willing to risk? When you're younger, it's easier to risk more, because you have less at stake. As you get older, however, you probably want to provide for your family, which means you might want to be more conservative in your investments.

Many people talk about how you should allocate your investment portfolio. My point is just to understand your risk tolerance. If those ups and downs go up and down and you're getting sick every day, that's not great. For me, I have almost all of my money in retirement and my own business, because that's where I choose to focus. That's because I choose to live a lifestyle where I'm not only free in terms of time, energy, relationships, and money, but also in terms of less stress. I have automated systems in place, which can make me money even when I'm not working. If you set this up correctly, you'll be earning money for years, like creating your very own annuity. Plus, you're in command of the value you add, which means you control your own destiny.

Identify Excuses, Install Systems

Secret number ten to leverage your money is to *identify excuses and install systems to overcome those excuses.* Why do most businesses fail? Because they don't have the right systems in place. Any why not? Because they weren't trained properly.

In the first place, there's a ton of misinformation out there. In the second place, most of the great marketers may be great at marketing, persuading and selling, but they can't teach their way out of paper bag. That's why millions of entrepreneurs are either getting no advice or bad advice. When you're in that situation, it's much easier to fail than it is to succeed.

People often excuse themselves by saying they don't have the money in the bank to start a business.

I had $800 when I started, and it was a hundred times harder back then. There were no tools; it was like trying to build a house with rocks and sticks. I mean, it was rudimentary. So I had no money either, but I did it because I had a Why-To. When you find the why, you'll find the way.

WHEN YOU FIND YOUR WHY, YOU'LL FIND THE WAY.

Other people use the excuse that they have a family and can't devote the time needed to start and run a business. Yet many single moms are making a lot of money in their own home-based businesses. In fact, your family that can be your Why-To: "I want to spend more time with my family. I don't want to be on the road all the time, driving in an awful commute." Many clients have said that to me: "I realized I was spending my entire life in the car, away from my family." You can use that as a Why-Not-To, or as a Why-To.

Another excuse: "Noah, I never went to business school, so I don't know how to start and run a successful business."

Look, I didn't go to business school either. Heck, I was a professional ballet dancer who had no idea how to start an online business, let alone grow it to seven and eight figures.

Let me ask you a question: who are the teachers in business schools? Professors. Are these professors rich? No—because if they were rich, they probably wouldn't be teaching.

Now I'm not dissing professors or teachers. In fact, I have the greatest admiration for teachers! However, in business school, you're usually not taught how to run a successful business—the curriculum is usually about how to be a successful manager or business professional. In other words, most business schools teach how to be a successful employee, rather than a successful entrepreneur.

ASK THIS SIMPLE QUESTION TO DECIDE WHO YOU WANT TO COACH YOU.

Ask yourself, "Who would I rather have coach me—someone whose only success story is themselves, or someone who's helped thousands of other people like me to fulfill their dreams?" It's easy to find "gurus" whose only success story is themselves. That means, they're great at marketing and self-promotion, but they suck at teaching and coaching.

That's why the far more important question is: "Does this coach have a SYSTEM that anyone can follow to become successful, or is it all about that guru's personality?"

For example, have you ever gone to a guru-led seminar and discovered that they don't have anything new to say? That they're just telling stories and repeating clichés that don't really help you? That's the main difference between *personality-driven success* and *system-driven success*. Make sure you hire someone to coach you who has a proven system you can follow, not just a winning personality.

How to Stop Working 24/7

Perhaps you're thinking, "I'm tired of worrying about money, struggling to take time off, keeping up with competitors, and I'm constantly thinking about work and finding it difficult to relax or enjoy my personal time."

The fact is, these are just symptoms. The real problem is that you don't have the right systems in place, because you weren't taught how to do it. In fact, I spent more than half a million dollars over a period of twenty years to organize this system. That's much longer than it should have taken. I would pay a marketing guru a lot of money, only to find out they had one little nugget that I overpaid for.

If you're working fourteen hours a day, and your income is up and down, these are symptoms. They're not the cause. The cause is everything that I've been discussing in this book.

You can go online and type in, "How to make money in business." You'll find a gazillion videos, mostly from sketchy people. We don't know if we can trust them, and 99 percent of the time, we cannot. You need to find a coach, a mentor who has a long-term track record, not just for themselves, but for others.

For example, most gurus say, "I made all this money." All that proves is that you're good at selling and marketing. That doesn't mean you can teach; in fact, it often means the opposite. What is so concerning to me in this industry is that those guys are making a lot of money from unsuspecting people. My job now is to say, we're not going to take that anymore. We're not going to listen to these guys who have made money for themselves but haven't helped others. In short, you want to follow someone who has developed a system for success that *anyone* can use, and who has helped many others to overcome challenges, achieve their dreams and live the Freedom Lifestyle.

Afformations on Money

Here are my top ten Afformations for the Focus Factor of money.

1. Why am I so rich?
2. Why do I have more than enough money?
3. Why does my income always exceed my expenses?
4. Why do I live below my means?
5. Why do I know exactly where I'm going?
6. Why do I know why I want to get there?
7. Why do I get the right help and support?
8. Why is money so attracted to me?
9. Why do I plan my work and work my plan?
10. Why do I get to live The 7-Figure Life?

Noah's Note

Money is the first thing that most people think of when they hear The 7-Figure Life. My intention in this chapter is to show you that while money is indeed important, money is a by-product of having the right plan, the right tools, and the right support in place—and then taking the right actions.

I grew up poor in a rich neighborhood. Perhaps if I had grown up rich in a rich neighborhood, I wouldn't have figured out these systems to actually create true wealth, health and happiness.

Therefore, follow the secrets I gave you in this chapter to leverage your money, so that you too can life the Freedom Lifestyle of your dreams!

6

The Four Pillars of Transformation

Ensure Your 7-Figure Life for the Long Term

The final question has to do with long-term transformation. In other words, once you're employing the principles of The 7-Figure Life, how do you sustain your success over the long term, when the challenges come, the initial high wears off, and you're tempted to cut corners?

That's where my model of the four pillars of transformation comes in. To experience long-term, lasting transformation, you must employ these four pillars:

- The right plan: what to do.
- The right tools: how to do it.
- The right support: who's in your corner, believing in you?
- The right actions: you've got to actually implement your plan.

Building a happy 7-Figure Life is like building a house. You need the same four elements. You need to have the right plan: a blueprint. Here's what the house is going to look like. It's a two-dimensional representation of a three-dimensional house.

Then you need the right tools. What are the tools for building a house? Hammer, saw, nails, screwdriver, and so on. Then you need the right support: people in your corner believing in you.

When I was five years old, my father decided to build a house. He's a brilliant guy, a very hard worker, and he created the blueprint from his own brain. He didn't have any training. He didn't go to architectural school. He just figured out how to build a house. Actually, he had a good plan. He also had the right tools: a hammer, saw, nails, a screwdriver.

But my father never had that third element: the support that he needed. He didn't have the financial support. He didn't have support from his family. He didn't have people in his corner believing in him. That is the main reason we ended up losing the house. When I was fifteen, the bank foreclosed on us, and we had to move out of that house because my father couldn't finish it and couldn't make the payments. You can have a good plan and the right tools, but if you don't have the right support, it's going to be hard to finish your house and sustain it over the long term.

When people come to me, I show them what to do. I've given a lot of that in this book. I also give them the right tools: here's how to do it, here's how to employ the plan, here's how to implement it. Then, of course, I give you the right support: 90 percent of my work as a coach is believing in people, because they come to me wanting to believe, but they've been burned or traumatized, so they've lost their self-confidence. I'm able to believe in them even before they believe in themselves.

I give you the right plan, the right tools, and the right support. But there's one thing that I can't give you, and that is to take the right actions. To use a health analogy, you can hire me as a personal trainer to help you get in shape. I can tell you what to do, give you the exercises, the tools you need, and I'm believing in you. Then you say, "That's great, Noah, but I want you to do my sit-ups so I get six-pack abs." It would be nice if you could hire someone else to do your sit-ups for you, but unfortunately that doesn't work. I can give you everything else, but I can't give you the right actions, meaning I can't make you do anything. The people who are willing to take the action, who do the sit-ups, if you will, are the ones who get long-term, lasting, fulfilling transformation.

THIS IS THE ONE THING I CAN'T GIVE YOU.

After reading this book, you might be tempted to take what I've given you and try to put a plan together and do it on your own. Sure, it will take longer and you'll probably make a few costly mistakes along the way, but you could do it. However, if you want to *dramatically accelerate* your results and reach your goals up to ten times faster—getting in 12 weeks what would normally take you 12 months or more—then we can do it together.

You heard my story about deciding to hire a business coach when I was $40,000 in debt, because I want you to realize that even if you're facing tough times right now, you can get help. In fact, I could have listened to the people who said, "Ten years with nothing to show for it, you should quit." Instead, I decided to get help—and my life changed as a result of finally getting the *right* help.

The truth is that there's no such thing as an overnight success. For instance, if you're thinking, "I've been at this for a long time and I'm still not where I want to be," I hope that my story inspires you and helps you find the courage to keep going.

Fact is, even with my painfully slow start, I've still managed to create a 7-figure dream lifestyle as a result of implementing my own system. That means, if I can do it, you can do it too!

Of course it takes courage. The word *courage* comes from the Latin word *cor*, which means *heart*. In this book, I've talked about head trash. Notice I call it *head trash*, not *heart trash*. It's the voice in your head that says, "I can't do it. I'm not enough." I got through my difficulties because I was acting from my heart. When all the voices, all the messages said, "You can't do it," I said, "I'm going to do it. I want to do it, and I have to do it. Whatever it takes, I'm going to make this work." That was coming from courage.

Think about the people who act from courage every day: our servicemen and women, our police officers and firefighters, the brave men and women on the front lines of the pandemic. These people act from courage— their heart. A fireman's head may be saying, "You know what? I could die today. I might go into a burning building, and I could die." Why do they run into the burning building when everyone else is running away? Their head says, "Get out of here." But their heart says, "No, I'm doing this. I'm serving my community. I'm serving my fellow human beings." The same is true of our brave

THIS IS HOW TO MOVE FORWARD IN SPITE OF YOUR FEAR.

servicemen and women and health care workers. When I look at people like that, it humbles me to know that these people have great courage every day. Their head says, "You're crazy to do this; what if you die?" Their heart says, "I'm going anyway."

That's what inspired me to keep moving towards my goal when I was stuck in that basement. I needed help, I had paid for a lot of bad help, and I finally got the help that I needed. Now I'm privileged to be able to offer that same help to others. If you are facing a basement moment, know that there is help available. I've given you the right plan and the right tools in this book. We have the right support available, and you can take the right actions when you find your Why-To and when you act from courage—your heart.

For example, we have individual and group coaching programs for resourceful people who have outgrown the "conventional self-help wisdom" and want to gain exclusive, insider access to the exact system that's added more than $2.8 billion in new revenues for me and my clients since 1997.

Because I believe passionately in *system-driven success* (rather than personality-driven success), I give you the paint-by-numbers, plug-and-play, fill-in-the-blank checklists, blueprints, and templates, so you don't have to waste any more time and money trying to figure it out on your own.

We also have done-for-you services where we build your online sales funnels and help you create irresistible offers that you create once and sell forever, thereby freeing you from the "trading time for money" trap that so many entrepreneurs fall into.

Whether you want it done for you, done with you, or to do it yourself, we have all of those levels available at **NoahStJohn.com**, our main website. Please avail yourself of these tools so that you can accelerate your results up to ten times faster and you don't have to do it on your own anymore.

When I'm asked how I would like to be remembered when I have passed on, I remember a great quote from Woody Allen: "I don't want to achieve immortality through my work. I want to achieve it through not dying." Of course that's a joke: that's not going to happen. We are all going to pass on. In the game of life, Father Time is undefeated. So, yes, of course, I will pass on like everybody.

THIS IS HOW I'D LIKE TO BE REMEMBERED.

I think about this question every day, because I have faced death twice in my life. The first time was when I almost committed suicide. The second time was on a highway. My wife and I had just flown home from one of our events, and it was 1:00 a.m. in the morning. We had just flown into Cleveland Airport. There was a little light snow on the ground. We were all alone on a four-lane highway. All of a sudden, ahead of me I saw a pair of headlights coming directly at us in my lane, traveling in the wrong direction. In an instant, I thought to myself, "Is this really happening? Are those headlights really coming straight at us?" I swerved, and the other car went right by me at seventy miles an hour in the wrong lane. I looked at Babette and said, "Did you see that?" She said, "Yes." I said, "We could have just died."

Thank goodness she witnessed it, because I couldn't believe that it had just happened; I thought I'd imagined it. The fact is, we both would have been dead if I had taken my eyes off the road even for a moment.

The question is, *how would you like to be remembered?* When I ask my clients that question, most people answer that they want to be remembered as a good parent, a loving spouse, and someone who left the world a little bit better because they lived.

There's an old saying that success is knowing that even one life has breathed more easily because you have lived. For example, when I share my story of facing death twice, many people tell me, "I'm so glad you didn't die and I'm grateful that you're still here."

What about YOU?

What is the legacy you want to leave?

And what are you willing to do to make that legacy become reality?

Conclusion

"Einstein was a man who could ask immensely simple questions. And what his life showed, and his work, is that when the answers are simple too, then you hear God thinking."

—JACOB BRONOWSKI

I t was a dark and stormy night.

Aboard the mighty battleship *Missouri*, the captain and first officer stood on the bridge, looking out into the stormy seas. Suddenly, a light appeared in the distance through the thick fog. A ship was right in their path!

The captain said to the first officer, "Signal them to move to starboard."

"Aye-aye, Captain." Over the signal lamp, the signalman sent the message using Morse code, *Starboard.*

A few moments later, the signal came back, *Starboard yourself.*

"What!" the captain shouted. "Tell them who we are and tell them to move to starboard immediately!"

The signalman sent the message: *This is the mighty Missouri. Starboard!*

A few moments later, the signal came back: *This is the lighthouse. Your call.*

The principles and tools I've taught you in this book are like the lighthouse; they don't move. We can crash ourselves against them, or we can use them to guide our forward progress.

Now that this book is over, you can choose to go back to your old way of thinking; but why would you?

You now have the ultimate advantage, which means *starting right now*, you can change the trajectory of your life. Starting today, the choices you make and the actions you take will determine who you will be and where you'll end up for the rest of your life.

Therefore, don't put off creating and experiencing the happiness, health, wealth, success, and love that you desire. If you want your life to improve, you must improve yourself first. Starting right now, commit to implementing this process immediately, so you can begin to embody more of your potential than you ever imagined possible.

Imagine . . . just fourteen days from now, you will be well on your way to transforming every area of your life!

Let's Keep Helping Others

May I ask you a quick favor? If this book has added value to your life, if you feel like you're better off after reading it, I'm hoping you'll do something for someone you care about. Give this book to them. Let them borrow your copy. Ask them to read it so they have the opportunity to transform their life for the better.

Or, if you're not willing to give up your copy quite yet because you're planning on going back and re-reading it, you can get them their own copy.

It could be for no special occasion at all other than to say, "Hey, I love and appreciate you, and I want to help you live your best life. Read this."

If you believe, as I do, that being a great friend, family member, or colleague is about helping your friends and loved ones to become the best versions of themselves, I encourage you to share this book with them.

Together, we are truly elevating the consciousness of Earth, one question at a time.

Thank you so much!

For Those Who Want to Go Further and Faster

"If breaking a habit has been hard for you to do,
then a helping hand is in order."

—KENNETH SCHWARZ

When I discovered Afformations in April 1997, I knew that I had found something that would revolutionize the personal growth industry. Because The Afformations Method is so simple, yet so profound and transformational, I had a vision that millions of people around the world would one day be using my method.

The irony is, even though my vision was crystal clear in my mind, I didn't know how to achieve it. So, I kept searching and searching for how to make my vision a reality.

Then, on October 20, 1997, I made a second discovery that changed my life. I discovered the hidden condition that causes millions of people to hold themselves back from the success they're capable of. I called that condition *success anorexia* because millions of people are unknowingly and unconsciously *starving themselves of success*.

It was only after my second epiphany that I knew what I had to do—begin writing, coaching, and speaking about Afformations and success anorexia.

So that's what I did.

First came *Permission to Succeed*®.

Then *The Secret Code of Success*.

Then *The Book of Afformations*®.

Then *Power Habits*®.

And now, the book you're holding in your hands.

As a result, I became the only author in the history of publishing to have works published by Hay House, HarperCollins, Simon & Schuster, Mindvalley, Nightingale-Conant, and the *Chicken Soup for the Soul* publisher.

Through all of this, one fact became abundantly clear—as miraculous as Afformations are to change your life, we still need more. That's because we humans are complex creatures and because success itself is so varied and multi-layered.

I realized that to fulfill my mission of *elevating the consciousness of Earth, one question at a time*, I had to create a complete, all-encompassing system that would cover all areas of life, work, and how to achieve fulfillment, success, and self-mastery.

That's why I created programs like *Power Habits®️ Academy* and *The 12-Week Breakthrough*. These programs and others represent the culmination of my twenty-five years of coaching high achievers to enjoy even higher levels of success, happiness, and fulfillment.

Let me give you an analogy to illustrate the point. Let's say you decide one day that you want to buy a new house. You get into your car and start driving around the neighborhood you want to live in. Do you drive around and say, "Wow, look at all those nice foundations?"

No, you're looking at all the beautiful houses! In fact, you don't even notice the foundations. However, without a strong foundation, is your new house going to be solid? Nope, it's going to collapse because the foundation is the beginning of building a strong, solid house.

Therefore, if you'd like to go further even faster and build on the foundation you now have from this book, I highly recommend the following steps:

Step 1: Subscribe to my YouTube channel at **WatchNoahTV.com** because you'll discover my latest insights and best practices on Afformations, Power Habits, Inner Game and Outer Game Mastery, and a variety of other subjects to help you live a 7-Figure Life.

Step 2: Get my new report at **FreeGiftfromNoah.com** because you'll discover how I help my clients make more in just twelve weeks than they made in the previous twelve months, while gaining one to three hours per day and four to eight weeks per year.

Step 3: To accelerate your results even faster, schedule your free 7-Figure Breakthrough Session at **BreakthroughwithNoah.com** because you'll discover how my clients are instantly shattering their limiting beliefs that were putting a ceiling on their business revenue using one simple process that can take place in as little as five minutes a day . . . 100% guaranteed!

"Noah St. John's coaching starts where Think and Grow Rich *and* The Secret *left off!"*
—Mike Filsaime, 8-Figure CEO of Groove.cm

"My company went from being stuck at $4M in sales to over $20M in sales as a result of coaching with Noah!"
—Adam S., Eight-Figure CEO

"My income is up 800% since I started coaching with Noah!"
—Steven B., Entrepreneur

"Coaching with Noah enabled me to double my business in less than twelve months after I'd been stuck at the same level for fifteen years!"
—Aubrey R., Entrepreneur

"In the first two weeks of coaching with Noah, I TRIPLED my investment!"
—Thomesa L., Entrepreneur

"As a result of coaching with Noah, I doubled my income, then doubled it AGAIN in just 12 short weeks!"
—Mike C., Entrepreneur

Recommended
Resources

YOUR FREE BONUS GIFT

As a thank-you for purchasing this book, I would like to give you exclusive, insider access to the exact system my clients are using to instantly shatter their limiting beliefs that were putting a ceiling on their business revenue, once and for all, using ONE simple process that can take as little as five minutes a day.

Best of all, it works especially well even when all the other programs, seminars, methods, systems and gurus have let you down or you don't actually know what the specific problem is.

This is also the fastest and easiest way to gain special access to the lucrative system that's added more than $2.8 billion in revenue for me and my clients since 1997.

So if you . . .

- Want a proven system to instantly shatter limiting beliefs and recapture lost revenues
- Have a business that's beyond start-up phase and is actually making sales
- Are ready for "hockey stick growth" in your company
- Want insider access to my fill-in-the-blank templates, checklists and resources
- Want to know how this guaranteed system can work for you

Schedule your complimentary 7-Figure Breakthrough Session now, because we will review your business, see how this system can work for you, offer you some advice on how to use it, and then discuss (if we know we can help you) how we can help you implement it—GUARANTEED.

Book your 7-Figure Breakthrough Session now at
BreakthroughwithNoah.com

Book Noah to Speak

"Noah is definitely NOT your typical motivational speaker! I took six pages of notes during his keynote presentation. SIMPLY PHENOMENAL—A MUST-HAVE RESOURCE for every organization that wants to grow!"

—Mary Kay Cosmetics

"All I heard was great feedback! Thank you, Noah, for really engaging our audience. I am recommending you as a speaker for more meetings."

—Meeting Planners International

*"I highly recommend Noah St. John as a keynote
speaker because he resonates on a deep emotional
level with his audience. Dynamic, impactful,
inspiring, motivating, and professional—
in short, the PERFECT speaker!"*
—City Summit & Gala

Book Noah as your keynote speaker, and you're guaranteed to make your event highly enjoyable and unforgettable.

For more than two decades, Noah St. John has consistently rated as the #1 keynote speaker by meeting planners and attendees.

His unique style combines inspiring audiences with his remarkable TRUE story, keeping them laughing with his high-energy, down-to-earth style, and empowering them with actionable strategies to take their RESULTS to the NEXT LEVEL.

Book Noah for your event at
BookNoah.com

Also Available from Dr. Noah St. John

BREAKTHROUGH WITH NOAH

How I Help My Clients Make More in Just 12 Weeks
Than They Made in the Past 12 Months—
While Gaining 1–3 Hours per Day
and 4–8 Weeks a Year.
BreakthroughwithNoah.com

POWER HABITS® ACADEMY

Take Out Your Head Trash About Money,
Admit What You Truly Desire
and Experience Your Quantum Leap.
PowerHabitsAcademy.com

THE AFFORMATIONS® ADVANTAGE

Immediately Attract More Abundance on Autopilot.

Afformations.com

Shop our complete line of business and
personal growth programs:

ShopNoahStJohn.com

Book Noah to speak at your virtual or live event:

BookNoah.com

Motivate and Inspire Others!

"SHARE THIS BOOK"

RETAIL $24.95

Special Quantity Discounts Available

To Place an Order, Contact:

(330) 871-4331

info@SuccessClinic.com

Acknowledgments

My Most Grateful Thanks to . . .

God, the answer to all of our questions.

My beautiful wife, Babette, for being my best friend and the best Loving Mirror I've ever had. Thank you for believing in me and supporting me and for your tireless commitment to helping me put a dent in the universe.

My parents, who sacrificed and gave more than they had.

Jack Canfield, for grokking my message when it was a bunch of pages bound with a piece of tape.

Dr. Stephen R. Covey, who inspired me to get into the business of helping people when the audiocassette album of *The 7 Habits of Highly Effective People* fell off a church bookshelf and landed at my feet. I swear I'm not making that up.

Through the years, many have shared ideas, inspiration, mentoring, and support that have impacted my life, each in a different way. While it's impossible to thank everyone, please know that I appreciate you greatly:

Alex Mandossian, Arianna Huffington, Donny Osmond, Gary Vaynerchuk, Jenny McCarthy, Joel Osteen, John Lee Dumas, Marie Forleo, Suze Orman, Adam Farfan, Anik Singal, Ashley Grayson, Dr. Brad Nelson, Brian Kurtz, Chris Stoikos, Dan Bova, Daniel Marcos, David Meltzer, David Deutsch, Dr. Fabrizio Mancini, Glenn Morshower, Harvey Mackay, Jason Hewlett, Jay Abraham, Jeff Magee, Jeffrey Hayzlett, Jen Groover, JJ Virgin, Jim Kwik, Joe Polish, Joe Vitale, John Assaraf, John Cito, Dr. John Gray, Jon Benson, Kat Parker-Merritt, Dr. Kellyann Petrucci, Lisa Nichols, Mari Smith, MaryEllen Tribby, Mike Filsaime, Nathan Osmond, Neale Donald Walsch, Peter Hoppenfeld, Rich Schefren, Richard Rossi, Russell Brunson, Tom Junod, Walter O'Brien, Verne Harnish, and so many other people who have inspired me in my career!

Very special thanks to the vast and growing tribe of our phenomenal coaching clients around the world who believe in the power of this message. Thank you for spreading the word about my work to all corners of the globe!

Every day, as I hear more and more stories of how the coaching work we do together is changing lives, you inspire, encourage, and uplift me.

I am humbled by your stories of how my work has changed your lives—truly, more than you know. Whether you're a member of our Coaching Family, attend one of our virtual events or online trainings this year, or simply commit to telling your friends about this book, I'm grateful for you.

Every day brings with it the opportunity to be reborn in the next greatest version of ourselves.

NOW IT'S YOUR TURN

I LOOK FORWARD TO BEING A PART OF YOUR SUCCESS STORY!

About the Author

NOAH ST. JOHN, PhD is recognized as "The Father of AFFORMATIONS®" and "The Mental Health Coach to the Stars."

Working with Hollywood celebrities, seven- and eight-figure company CEOs, professional athletes, top executives, and elite entrepreneurs, Noah is famous for helping his coaching clients make more in twelve weeks than they did in the previous twelve months, while gaining 1–3 hours per day and 4–8 weeks a year.

Noah's clients are the 0.1% rock stars who love to *take action* and get amazing *results!*

Noah is also the only author in history to have works published by HarperCollins, Hay House, Simon & Schuster, Mindvalley, Nightingale-Conant, and the *Chicken Soup for the Soul* publisher. His eighteen books have been published in nineteen languages worldwide.

Noah's mission is to eliminate not-enoughness from the world, and he is internationally known for his signature coaching services and facilitating workshops at companies and institutions across the globe. Noah delivers private workshops, virtual events, and online courses that his audiences call "MANDATORY for anyone who wants to succeed in life and business."

One of the most requested, in-demand business and motivational keynote speakers in the world, Noah is famous for having "The Midas Touch" because his clients have added more than $2.8 billion in found revenues. His sought-after advice is known as the "secret sauce" to business and personal growth.

He also appears frequently in the news worldwide, including ABC, NBC, CBS, FOX, The Hallmark Channel, National Public Radio, *Chicago Sun-Times*, *Parade*, *Los Angeles Business Journal*, *The Washington Post*, *Woman's Day*, *Entrepreneurs on Fire*, *Selling Power*, Entrepreneur.com, *The Jenny*

McCarthy Show, Costco Connection, and *SUCCESS* magazine.

Fun fact: Noah once won an all-expenses-paid trip to Hawaii on the game show *Concentration*, where he missed winning a new car by three seconds. (Note: He had not yet discovered his Afformations® Method or Power Habits® Formula.)

Book Noah to speak for your next virtual or live event, conference or seminar at **BookNoah.com**.

CPSIA information can be obtained
at www.ICGtesting.com
Printed in the USA
JSHW030329070223
37361JS00003B/3